What others are saying . . .

"When Sharon Rezac Andersen, my UND colleague, returned from Nicaragua in 1983, I heard her true story. It has influenced my reporting of facts and challenged me more deeply to search for truth wherever it can be found. Rezac Andersen should have been a journalist. Her story demonstrates a passion for truth that inspires us all."

—Mike Jacobs, editor, *Grand Forks Herald*

"In this honest and personal memoir, Sharon Rezac Andersen recounts the truth-seeking journey she and other women made to Nicaragua in the 1980s, giving us new insights into that troubled place and time and reminding us that truth always confers both liberation and responsibility."

—Glenda Martin and Mollie Hoben, cofounders, *Minnesota Women's Press*

"The Truth—written and lived by one who knows the definition."

—Doris C. Steffy, author of *Mrs. Steffy: Our Mother, the Mortician*

The Burden *of* Knowing

A journey, a friendship, and the power of truth in Nicaragua

Sharon Rezac Andersen

Gene thank you for your comments and taking this journey with me.

Shalom – Sharon

The Burden of Knowing: A journey, a friendship,
and the power of truth in Nicaragua

Published by Wheatmark®
1760 East River Road, Suite 145, Tucson, Arizona 85718 U.S.A.
www.wheatmark.com

ISBN: 978-1-60494-804-2
LCCN: 2012937932

Acknowledgments

This book was made possible by the support of so many people.

First, I want to thank my parents, Julia and Frank Rezac, who instilled in me the value of education and reading and an appreciation for all humankind. Though departed from this earth, Mom and Dad remain with me always.

My late German-Russian immigrant grandmother, Margaret, who told me from childhood, "Never let anyone name for you an enemy!" I hope my mind remains as stimulated as hers was at age ninety-seven.

Margie, my life mentor, whose constant insistence on working for peace with justice preempted the birthing of this book, written in her memory. I hope I have done you justice, dear friend.

My life partner, Gary Andersen. You've been with me every moment of my adult-life quest. Your commitment to sharing our fulfilled lives as equal partners has made my extraordinary life opportunities possible. I am grateful for our forty-eight years as best friends and lovers—of each other and of our family.

Our children, Mark, Kelly, and Josh, who have always provided me with the love and support needed while on my life journey. Each time I watch you and your spouses lovingly parent our grandchildren, I recognize life's greatest reward.

Dear friends Glenda Martin, Mollie Hoben, Doris Steffy, Betty Everett, and Pat Lamb, who have read and reread *The Burden of Knowing* many times. Your honest insights, suggestions, and constructive criticism have been valued along with your friendships that I'll cherish a lifetime.

My University of North Dakota international students who embraced this fact: "We are all Earth's family, and though we live and pray and celebrate in different ways, we are linked by a common dream—peace. Beautiful peace on Earth." You have taught me so much about the world.

Many university colleagues have been instrumental in the writing of this book. Dr. George Frein, my academic advisor during undergraduate studies in world religion and philosophy, guided me, as an older-than-average student, on a quest toward seeking truth, including an appreciation for people of all cultures, philosophies, and world religions. I also appreciate the humanities scholars you brought to people in the tents during Chautauqua.

Dr. Sherry O'Donnell and Dr. Sandy Donaldson, professors in women's studies, who introduced me to the "herstory" of women such as Abigail Adams, Louisa May Alcott, Maya Angelou, Susan B. Anthony, Emily Dickinson, Margaret Fuller, Elisabeth Cady Stanton, Sojourner Truth, and numerous others. Thank you!

Dr. Steve Rendahl, Director of UND communication, who was instrumental as my advisor in graduate studies and taught the importance of quality oral and written communication and the value of public discourse.

Friends, for your continuous encouragement while writing this book: Dr. Dan and Shirley Goodwin, Gwen Crawford, Bernie Schumacher, and all the people who have traveled my life journey on various occasions.

To the martyrs, heroes, AMNLAE, and our study guides in Nicaragua, for a life experience I'll always remember. *Muchas gracias!*

With gratitude to the Wheatmark staff for the editing and enhancement of this book.

And to you, the readers, with hope that *The Burden of Knowing* awakens in you a search for truth—a truth, I suggest, that only comes from factual information, multiple resources, engaged in-depth conversations, cultural understanding, and reading the great books. Heartfelt thanks to each of you for traveling this journey with me.

"We cannot begin to understand another person's experience until we have asked the right questions of our own."

—Sheila Collins, "Theology in the Politics of Appalachian Women"

Preface

What is truth? Do we create our own reality and live within those confines while expecting others to live according to our values and standards, or are we open to other people's opinions and perspectives? This book asks the question "What is truth, where do we find it, and will truth transform our lives?"

For each of us, our journey toward truth will be a lifetime adventure. I welcome you as a traveler on your own life journey. While you sojourn with me, I invite you to meet the people and places that have influenced my life—while *you* recall the persons who have journeyed with you through *yours.*

The Burden of Knowing was born during my study in Nicaragua. This story is true: I have seen the corpses of slain youths in their caskets. I have wept alongside the coffins with the mothers and fathers of these young heroes and martyrs. Traveling with a study group, I went from city to countryside seeking truth. Have you heard about the massacre in Nicaragua?

On this journey, will we travel on bumpy roads? Of course! But together, we will stop to shake off the dust and continue toward wherever the path leads us. Life is not always easy, is it?

I suggest that to experience a sense of truth in oneself is to understand that we are part of a greater wholeness, which is our world, the whole human family. I learned this fact as academic advisor to international students at the University of North Dakota. Yes, everyone is connected!

My hope is that after reading *The Burden of Knowing*, each of us will examine more than one source for accurate information. I suggest to all readers that media "infotainment" has no merit or validity when trying to determine what is true.

Seeking truth while writing *The Burden of Knowing*, I reflected on living a country life on a Hubbard Prairie farm during childhood to moving into a small Minnesota town as a teenager. I journeyed through a life of marriage and raising children in Grand Forks, North Dakota, as well as working for two years in Manhattan. I studied in Cuba and Nicaragua and graduated from the University of North Dakota, launching my career as director of the UND International Centre. Would I change any of my life choices or experiences? No, not one!

Completing a master's degree in communication, traveling on study tours, and working with international students have helped me focus more clearly on my own life paradigm—how I perceive, understand, and interpret the world from my own lens. Visions of the self and deliberation about the concept of an inner core have given way to the consideration of the collective. I believe we create our identity through relationships with others. For me, that reality mandates understanding and celebrating cultural diversity while becoming relational within the global community.

Traveling this journey, let us focus together on broader units of being. Our sojourn will take us from individualism to a worldview of relational reality. Therefore, the "I" so predominant today will be replaced with a "we," modeled after our past generations.

As you read about my Nicaraguan experience, my hope is that you, too, will accept the concept that it is much more difficult to be accountable for your behavior within a group, society, or world than it is to be accountable solely to yourself.

The Making of a Martyr

Each of us, on our journey through life, needs a mentor, a loyal friend, an adviser, someone who walks with us to celebrate the good times and paves our path to struggle through the difficult moments. Life isn't always easy is it?

In 1979, Sister Margie Tuite, a woman for whom social justice was a way of life, became my dear friend, confidant, and unique mentor. I met Margie when serving on the Church Women United National Board of Managers. She had come to our meeting to interview for the position of national director of Church Women United (CWU) Ecumenical Citizen Action. I was over-whelmed with her presence: Sr. Margie Tuite, a person bigger than life, with an infectious smile, a hearty laugh, and a loving personality, and with an obvious frustra-tion when she articulated her concerns for peace with justice in the world.

Margie's resume was impressive: She had earned a master's degree in English at Fordham University, New York; a master's degree in theology at Manhattan-ville College in Purchase, New York; and a doctorate in ministry at St. Mary of the Lake Seminary in Mundelein, Illinois. She taught social-justice dimensions of ministry at the Jesuit School of Theology in Chicago and summer sessions in major US colleges. In the 1960s, she served as a high school principal and teacher in Harlem Catholic schools, when she became active in the civil rights movement.

During the interview, when Margie was asked to describe herself, she explained the direction her life had taken: "As I look back, my own journey of struggle and deep commitment to justice began in my parents' walk-up apartment on Manhattan's east side. It concretized in a tall, shy, young woman crossing the bridge at Selma, Alabama. It found its greatest hope in the poor of Central America and their revolution. I have stayed in the struggle in spite of the long loneliness of the cosmic weariness."

Our board was aware of Margie's accomplishments. Margie was a leading voice for women's equality in the Roman Catholic Church, an advocate for the poor, and an educator on a broad range of social-justice issues. She had played a prominent role in the civil rights, peace, and women's movements as an activist, educator, organizer, and author. She was extremely well qualified for the position of national director of Church Women United Ecumenical Citizen Action.

When she was hired, her major responsibilities were to educate the CWU constituency on issues of peace with justice, provide training related to legislative and political strategies to advance CWU policies and resolutions, and work cooperatively with the Church Women United staff. In 1979, at the time of Margie's hiring, the twenty-one hundred local and fifty state units of Church Women United, making up the largest ecumenical movement in the United States, were working on issues such as the ratification of the Equal Rights Amendment, the rural financial farm crisis, the feminization of poverty, and systemic causes of classism, racism, sexism, and war.

Margie and I became close friends from the beginning of her tenure with CWU. We discovered immediately that we espoused the same values. Her leadership helped Church Women United make the connection between the individual and collective responsibility that mandated education, service, advocacy, and systemic change. I appreciated her wisdom; her ability to relate to and educate the twenty-six denominations and faith groups that supported CWU; and her constant work that mandated enhancing the human condition, working for the common good, and advocating peace with justice.

For me and the huge number of people with whom she worked, Sr. Margie Tuite embodied a faith-filled, "wide-awake woman" in a world that had unjustifiably fallen asleep. She continued to remind us, "I am pleading for peace but running out of time." It is an honor for me to share these components of her life. To you, my dear friend Margie, I dedicate *The Burden of Knowing.*

The Burden of Knowing

*M**y** life changed forever* after my forty-first birthday, January 1983. It was early morning. I was nestled in a chaise lounge sipping coffee, book in hand, when the telephone rang. The call was from my dear friend, Dominican Sister Margie Tuite.

"Happy birthday, Sharon! I wish I could be there to celebrate with you! I know your family will make it a love-filled day." Then her voice took a more serious tone. "I've been asked by Edna McCallion, consultant for Church Women United on United Nations Non-Governmental Affairs, to direct a study in Nicaragua. I want you to come with me."

I was shocked by her request. "Margie, Nicaragua is at war! Couldn't the trip be life threatening for us?"

"Yes, Nicaragua is at war. That is why you and I must go! This study is a two-week fact-finding mission related to the atrocities we've heard reported daily. Our responsibility will be to study the country, determine what is true, and communicate the facts when we return home. We need not worry about our lack of Spanish proficiency. My friends, Maryknoll Sisters living in

Nicaragua, will be our guides and our Spanish inter-preters throughout the entire study. They are working there to help end the bloodshed and suffering while advocating a nonmilitary-negotiated settlement of the Nicaraguan war."

I sank back in my chair. "I will talk it over with Gary when he arrives home. I'll call you tomorrow morning, Margie."

"Sharon, tell Gary that if a bullet comes, I'll place my 190-pound body over yours!"

That evening, as we celebrated my birthday, I told my family that Margie had invited me to study in Nicaragua. Alarmed by the news, Gary stood and put his arms around me.

"But won't your life be in danger? The media are reporting war and daily casualties in Nicaragua!"

I looked at our three children and asked them, "Are you afraid?" Josh, our eight-year-old, responded, "I feel safe. I'm not afraid of war, Mom, because I know you're always working for peace." As we embraced, Gary's and my eyes filled with tears.

That evening, as Gary and I discussed the study tour, I assured him I was not afraid to go to Nicara-gua. I told him, "Margie's friends, Maryknoll Sisters in Nicaragua, our guides and interpreters, will help keep us safe. Margie said to tell you that if a bullet comes toward me, she'll put her 190-pound body over mine."

Gary listened intently to my pleading voice. "I'll telephone my parents to see if they can move in with us during your absence, so someone is here while I'm at work." When his mom and dad agreed to move in the entire time I'd be gone, we all felt relieved. I was grateful for Gary's parents' generosity.

Margie, director of Church Women United Citizen Action, had received the request at her New York office. The Nicaragua study had been designed by CWU United Nations staff with Margie as their consultant. Margie had previously traveled to Nicaragua, invited there by missionary friends, Maryknoll Sisters and Jesuit priests, who, since the revolution, were working throughout the country as educators, theologians, and human-rights advocates. Following her return to the United States, she determined that accurate media information relating to the civil war taking place in Nicaragua was difficult to obtain. Most news reports in the media reflected the position of the US administration, which unconditionally condemned the Sandinista government. Her friends supported the advancements orchestrated by the Sandinista government since the 1979 revolution.

Her former experience in Nicaragua with the Maryknoll missionaries, her position as CWU staff for Ecumenical Citizen Action, and her concern that US administration and Central Intelligence Agency (CIA) reports were not accurate, made Margie a prime candidate to direct the study. She was elated to be asked.

Founded during wartime in 1941, Church Women United in the United States had engaged millions of women, representing twenty-six supporting denominations and faith groups, to study issues and take action on behalf of peace with justice in the world. With an office at 475 Riverside, New York, the United Nations, and Washington, DC, CWU had historically studied issues, provided information to the public, taken action for the common good, and made a huge impact on public opinion and policy. The task for *this* CWU study group was to find the truth about the civil war taking place in Nicaragua. We were to determine the disparity between what human-rights advocates—including Maryknoll missionaries—had reported about the progress of the Sandinista government since the 1979 Nicaraguan Revolution, compared to what the US president, Congress, State Department, and CIA had consistently articulated and written.

I knew the trip would be dangerous. However, it seemed important to me that I go on this fact-finding mission. Concerns of a secret, covert war in Nicaragua had escalated among faculty and students in the mass-media communication classes I was enrolled in at the University of North Dakota. The majority of staff and students believed that the "undeclared war" escalating in Nicaragua—funded by the United States—was killing innocent victims, undermining the newly established Sandinista government, and depleting the US economy. There was fear that Nicaragua could become another Vietnam.

I respected Margie's prominent role in the civil rights, peace, and women's movements. While serving on the CWU Citizen Action Committee, she had taught me volumes about studying and working on behalf of peace with justice. I had witnessed her ability to collect worldwide information and provide an enormous amount of resources to fifty states and 2,100 local Church Women United units. She consistently worked to help people make informed decisions on political issues.

In preparation for our trip, Margie sent volumes of

orientation materials to acquaint me with Nicaragua's history, the 1979 revolution, and current realities; I spent hours reading. Historically, I began to understand the hardships of the Nicaraguan peasants: Under the forty-year dictatorship of longtime president General Anastasio Somoza Debayle, the majority of Nicaraguan people lived in abject poverty—except for the Somoza family and their heirs. In 1979, the Sandinistas, representative of the poor Nicaraguan peasants, overthrew the Somoza dynasty. The US policy following the revolution was to encourage the Sandinista government to keep its pledge of pluralism and democracy. However, the Sandinistas became increasingly anti-American. They feared that, for many years, the United States had been supportive of the Somoza Government and was currently aligned with the Nicaraguan Somoza elite. Due to US and Somoza past history, the Sandinistas doubted if the United States could be trusted. The Sandinistas turned toward Cuba and the Soviet Union, who agreed to send volunteers to help with the Nicaraguan Literacy Campaign while also providing political, military, and economic assistance. Fearing that Nicaragua was being influenced by communism, the United States began supporting the Nicaraguan contras, who were Somoza former National Guard, armed opponents of the newly formed Sandinista government.

Although in 1983, the US president, with funds appropriated by Congress, continued to clothe, feed, and supervise the contras, US opinion polls indicated that a majority of the American public was not supportive. Opponents of the administration's policy feared that US involvement with the contras would embroil the United States into another Vietnam. Supporters of the policy feared that, without US support for the contras, the Soviets and Cubans would gain a dangerous vantage in Central America.

The task for our study group was to determine what was true: What military involvement, funding, or supplies had the United States provided for the contras' forces, working against the newly established Nicaraguan Sandinista government? Was Nicaragua becoming a communist country or a threat to the United States? Was the Sandinista government, since the 1979 revolution, working as a democracy? What was causing the civil war within Nicaragua?

Upon returning to the states, it was our responsibility as US citizens to report facts to our government, the media, the American citizenry, the Church Women United constituency, and the United Nations.

Four months later, in May 1983, I left Grand Forks, North Dakota, on the sojourn of a lifetime. Saying good-bye to my family and friends at the airport had been difficult; however, I was looking forward to this educational adventure.

The study group included thirty-one American women. Margie coordinated all arrangements; the first meeting was at the Miami airport. Collectively, we represented sixteen states, with a variety of educational, cultural, and socioeconomic backgrounds. Our ages ranged from twenty-three to seventy-two. The group included, among others, four Catholic nuns, two Protestant pastors, one television reporter, one newspaper editor, six Spanish interpreters, one legislative representative, and members of the Church Women United

Citizen Action Committee. Margie introduced each of us and gave us a brief orientation before we boarded our flight to Nicaragua. As our airplane ascended into the air, I was happy to be sitting next to Margie.

Arriving in Nicaragua

I awakened to the sound of wheels hitting the tarmac. I must have dozed throughout the long, nine-hour flight. I'd been extremely excited as our plane left Miami, stopped for a one-hour layover in Belize, and refueled in Honduras. Now we were finally in Nicaragua! A new adventure! What would we find? How could I write and communicate the truth?

I shook my sleeping friend sitting next to me. "Margie, wake up! We're in Nicaragua! Look, why are the flags flying half-mast?" We both wondered what tragedy the country had experienced now.

As we walked down the steps of the Tan-Sahsa airplane, we were surrounded by armed soldiers. I was astonished by the young ages of these military officials. Four Maryknoll nuns greeted us. Margie asked them, "Why are the flags flying half-mast?" One of the nuns responded, "That is what we want you to witness."

Friends of Margie's, the nuns quickly swept us from the tarmac. They ushered us to the Plaza de la Revolución (Revolution Plaza) where a huge crowd of people were gathered. The plaza was surrounded with caskets.

Margie and I were aghast! Wailing mothers wearing their kitchen aprons, eyes red and swollen, stood next to the caskets. I glanced inside the open casket closest to me and saw a young boy. His name, "José," was handwritten and taped on the end of his coffin. Next to José was a young girl; "Luisa" was the label handwritten and taped on her coffin. They looked like angels experiencing a peaceful sleep.

I thought of my son, Mark, fifteen years old, and my daughter, Kelly, fourteen—about the same ages of José and Luisa. The young people in the caskets beside me were just children, like my own. Wouldn't they have been the hope of their country's future? I glanced at Margie. Her mouth was open, but she did not speak. Tears flowed from her eyes. I whispered, "Margie, what do you think happened to these youths?"

She shook her head. "I don't know. Maybe this is why we are here. What have I gotten you into?"

The nuns who had met us at the airport informed our study group that the youths in the caskets were war casualties, killed by contra revolutionaries the evening before. The gathered crowd was paying their respects to the families during this memorial service. As we shared the grief with the families, we recognized that the event was more than a funeral. Our guides stated that the memorial service gave the Nicaraguan people an opportunity to renew their commitment to an ongoing struggle: their revolution. Daniel Ortega, defense minister of the Nicaraguan Sandinista government, spoke angrily from a loudspeaker.

"Our flags you see flying half-mast are to honor our slain youth!" He then denounced the US government. "These fallen youths were killed last evening by contras armed with ammunition supplied by the United States!" He consoled the mothers and fathers of the heroes. "Your daughters and sons did not die in vain! They are counted among the heroes and martyrs who have protected our country from the evil contra forces!"

Margie and I stood there shocked. I wondered if this was the truth we were seeking.

Defense Minister Ortega continued. "These high school student volunteers were ambushed and killed last night by counter-revolutionary forces, while protecting coffee crops along the Honduran-Nicaraguan border. When we sell coffee, our country's major export crop, we enhance our Nicaraguan economy. Contras, opposed to our revolution and Sandinista government, burn the crops at night to destabilize the Nicaraguan economy and divert energies from the vital task of rebuilding our country. Each night, we send a group of young, armed volunteers to the Honduran-Nicaraguan border to protect coffee crops from burning by the contras. As you are aware, this is not our first incident of slayings. Unfortunately, our young volunteers are not as militarily skilled as the contra forces. Parents, I am sorry for the deaths of your innocent victims. They are forever our country's heroes."

Following the memorial service, we left the plaza, unable to control our mourning. Exhausted, our study group boarded a bus provided for us by the Nicaraguan women's committee, AMNLAE. Twenty minutes later, we arrived at our living quarters: an abandoned motel. "This location is a safer place" our guides told us. Once our rooms were assigned, we went directly inside, too tired to debrief. Conversation had been minimal since the memorial service.

That evening, nestled in our small, cloistered room, hopefully protected from the outside world, Margie tossed and turned in her cot. She sat up, looked over at me, and saw I was also awake. "Sharon, do you know that our tax dollars paid for the killing of these youths?"

"Yes, I know, Margie!"

Our conversation, and the reality of standing at the caskets forever awakened in me "the burden of knowing."

"Perhaps travel cannot prevent bigotry, but by demonstrating that all peoples cry, laugh, eat, worry, and die it can introduce the idea that if we try and understand each other, we may even become friends."

—Maya Angelo

...icide (standing second from right) with other contra commanders. Deadly ambushes and worries about support from Washing...

INTERNATIONAL

The Secret War Boils Over

Concretizing the Burden

The next morning, the shrill sounds of crowing roosters outside my window woke me from a sound sleep. I looked over at Margie's cot; it was empty. I was frightened. Where had she gone this early in the morning without me? Didn't she know I would be fearing a contra attack after what we had witnessed at the memorial service?

Then the outside door to our living quarters creaked open. Nervously shaking from fright, I jumped out of my cot. Margie entered. She had gone to use the outdoor bathroom. She cleared her throat, crossed her arms, then leaned against my cot and announced gleefully, "There is no hot water this morning. We'll have to wait until evening to shower."

Her carefree demeanor made me smile. I responded, "I'll take a sponge bath like my mother commanded my sister, brother, and me. Mom always reminded us to wash up as far as possible, down as far as possible, and don't forget possible." Margie's laugh echoed throughout our tiny room. That was the first time I'd seen her smile or heard her laugh since we'd arrived in Nicaragua.

"Today's orientation begins in one hour. We'll join the other women for breakfast in fifteen minutes. Can you be ready?" Margie asked. I was looking forward to reuniting and communicating with the American women in the study group. We had not debriefed since the memorial service. Those of us with limited Spanish proficiency would meet the nuns assigned to be our guides and interpreters at each event throughout the study. Margie had informed us during our orientation in Miami that to remain safe, our itinerary would have to be planned on a daily basis. Following breakfast, we would be informed of today's itinerary.

Over breakfast, our group discussed the current political unrest in Nicaragua. We realized that war in the country was due largely to the revolutionary struggle that included the United States funding and arming the contra forces.

Margie stood and spoke in a stern voice. "We need to recognize and acknowledge the truth. The contra revolutionary forces are supported by US funds and weapons. I hope that the Nicaraguan people we encounter will separate us from our government!"

After breakfast, Margie acquainted us with her friends, the four Maryknoll nuns, who had ushered us from the tarmac. Bilingual, these American Catholic sisters each morning would provide our study group's orientation for the day's itinerary. Including the six Spanish-speaking women who were translators in our study group, we had ten Spanish interpreters. During orientation, the nuns welcomed us to Nicaragua then stated, "We decided to live in Nicaragua because we believe it fulfills our faith commitment to work with the poor, advocate for human rights, help with the literacy campaign, and teach Liberation Theology."

They told us that their political consciousness was heightened by working with the literacy campaign, health centers, the women's group AMNLAE, and teaching Liberation Theology. One of the nuns stated, "As people of faith, the personal is political in our daily lives. You'll experience that same reality in the Nicaraguan people as you travel from city to the countryside. The Nicaraguan people are a revolutionary people. Since the 1979 revolution, the majority have worked hard to create their country's identity; not a country ruled by communism, but a pluralistic form of government with shared leadership and responsibility." She paused then continued. "We are aware that the US government has portrayed Nicaragua as a communist country; in fact, that is the reason the US military is involved in the civil war here: to protect Nicaragua from communism. Nicaragua is no threat to the United States. Nicaragua is neither your enemy nor a communistic country!"

A member of the CWU Citizen Action Committee responded, "I want to show you two magazines I brought from the United States." She read the articles. One article, in a November 1982 issue of *Newsweek*, reported that the United States, through the CIA, had contributed nineteen million dollars for a covert operation carried out to undermine the newly established Nicaraguan Sandinista government. The US government had allied itself with the Somoza supporters, the contras. Contras set up camps in Honduras and were invading Nicaragua across the border. The whole operation was being directed from the US embassy in Honduras. A March 1983 issue of the *Washington Post* gave positive evidence that the contra forces were well equipped militarily by the United States, which was supplying the money and arms for the contras, as well as logistical support and communication equipment. The *Newsweek* and *Washington Post* articles provided additional evidence that the US government was providing military aid to the contra forces. The articles concretized the information Defense Minister Ortega had articulated at the memorial service: the United States was responsible for the deaths of those young high school students.

Reacting to the *Newsweek* and *Washington Post* articles, Margie rose to her full, majestic, six-foot height. "During former trips to Nicaragua, I worked in solidarity with local groups. While here, my friends introduced me to educators, community leaders, governmental officials, theologians, and women's groups. I have also met with mothers of the heroes and martyrs throughout the country, like those we saw mourning their slain loved ones at the memorial service. They have lost sons and daughters in this undeclared war. We'll have an opportunity to meet with similar groups during our study and become well informed about the current realities within Nicaragua. As these *Newsweek* and *Washington Post* articles inform us, I guarantee what you see, hear, and experience will be different than what you have read and heard in the US media or from our government. This study experience will become a burden to take back home!"

The tensions within our group began to mount. The information in the articles made us recognize the difficult work ahead of us: the responsibility to hear the voices of the Nicaraguan people and discern the truth of their experiences within the revolutionary struggle. The nuns proudly announced that we were the first all-women's group to study in Nicaragua since the 1979 revolution, and the first group to be hosted by the Nicaraguan's Women's Association, AMNLAE.

AMNLAE was named in memory of Luisa Amanda Espinoza. Luisa had been the first woman killed defending her family from an attack by troops of the Somoza family, Nicaragua's forty-year dictators. AMNLAE, with a membership of thirty thousand women, played significant roles in the revolution. One of the nuns stated that the Nicaraguan women, along with the men, became trained and armed to defend their country. They worked with illiteracy brigades, founded recovery centers for ex-prostitutes, and formed coalitions to establish health and childcare centers. Their goal was to create a Nicaraguan pluralistic society, void of the oppressive hierarchical Somoza dictatorship they had experienced prior to the 1979 revolution. AMNLAE achieved its goals by working with the support and cooperation of the Sandinista government, which was completely opposite from the dictatorial power and control they experienced under Somoza. They instituted a shared leadership to achieve empowerment for all and utilized a consensus model of decision making, instead of the pre-revolutionary hierarchical decision-making process. They advocated integration of *all* the people, instead of the Somoza style that had catered solely to the elite; they mandated equality as a right, instead of the inequality they had experienced under the former dictatorship; and they worked to provide for basic human needs to enhance the lives of all Nicaraguans.

Margie responded, "AMNLAE women's group is a strong advocate for human rights and justice in this country. That is why my friends, the Maryknoll Sisters, work cooperatively with them."

Margie introduced us to Doris Tijerino, director of AMNLAE. Doris, face scarred from torture by the Somoza National Guard during the revolutionary struggle, told us AMNLAE would provide our local transportation, lodging, and any needs requests. She stated, "While in our country, we want you to travel from city to countryside to meet our leaders and experience the lives of our people. We are proud of the advancements since the 1979 revolution. Today, you will learn about the benefits of our literacy campaign. We do not ask that you defend the revolution. Please, just go home and tell the truth about what you've seen and experienced while here."

I thought, *After what we witnessed at the memorial service yesterday, how can we deny them this?*

"*I* swore never to be silent whenever and wherever human beings endure suffering and humiliation. We must always take sides. Neutrality helps the oppressor, never the victim. Silence encourages the tormentor, never the tormented."

—Elie Wiesel

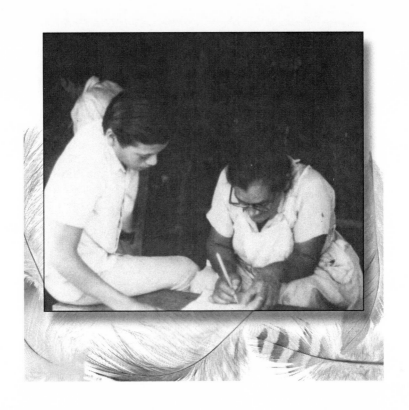

The Literacy Campaign

Following the meeting with Doris Tijerino and a brief orientation about the literacy campaign, our study group, guides, and interpreters traveled by bus to the Managua Education Center. As an educator, Margie was extremely interested to learn about the Nicaragua Literacy Campaign. We were welcomed to the Managua Education Center by the minister of education, Maryknoll Father Fernando Cardenal. He invited us to meet his students.

Sitting in one of the classrooms, Fernando told us, "Prior to 1979, 50 percent of our population over six years of age was illiterate. Fifteen days after the revolution, I began a monumental task: with the support of the Sandinista government, I organized sixty thousand volunteers who went into the mountains to teach reading skills, science, health, and math to the people. Now, three years later, the illiteracy rate has dropped from 50 percent to 12 percent." A smile covered his entire face as he proudly introduced his thirty students currently enrolled in the educational program. Their ages ranged from six to senior citizens.

Margie asked the students, "What has the literacy campaign done for you?"

An elderly woman smiled then replied, "I feel a new pride and respect for myself. I wrote a poem titled 'Notebooks' after I learned to read. May I read it to you?"

Placing a finger on each word, with confidence, she read us this poem in Spanish:

Your notebooks
In the health brigades
I see you
With your notebooks
Where for the first time
You wrote my name
After the alphabetization campaign.

We were intrigued to witness the pride of this senior citizen who finally had an opportunity to receive an education. I thought of how we take education for granted in our country.

Another student rose from her desk. She looked at each of us with assurance then proudly stated, "The literacy campaign helped me understand our history. Now we know how we can be the subjects, not the *objects*, of our history in the future."

Fernando further explained the education program's successes. "Most of our textbooks have come free from Germany and Sweden, countries that support our revolution and educational goals. A group of us translated the books into Spanish. We have 13,400 teachers, compared to ten thousand prior to the revolution. Today, over half of the country is enrolled in some educational program. The number of university students has increased one and one-half times. These are the goals the Sandinista government is trying to achieve. We believe education is the right of all Nicaraguans."

We were astounded by the literacy progress and Fernando's determination to educate all of the Nicaraguan people. The two-hour discussion helped us understand the Sandinista government's role in funding the literacy campaign for the benefit of Nicaragua's citizens. We left the education center knowing how the 1979 revolution and Sandinista government, in only four years, had made education a priority that enabled such a huge increase in literacy rates.

That night, Margie and I discussed the literacy campaign. I told her that when I had gone as one of the twelve CWU delegates from the US to Matanzas, Cuba, to attend a worldwide meeting as part of the Decade for Women, I lived with Dora Arce Valentin, host of the Decade for Women Conference. Dora informed me about the Nicaraguan Literacy Campaign. As educators and co-directors of the Matanzas Ecumenical Seminary, Dora and her partner Sergio Arce, an ordained pastor, helped Fernando Cardenal assemble and train the literacy-campaign volunteers in Nicaragua. I continued my story.

"While in Cuba, I interacted with women from around the world on issues related to human development, equality, educational systems, governmental procedures, and peace initiatives. During a plenary session, one of our US delegates addressed the Central

American women with these words, 'What can US women do to enhance the lives of women in Third World countries?'

"One of the participants, who represented Mexico, became livid! She stood and responded to our US delegation in anger: 'What do you mean "Third World country"? If we're "Third World," does that make the United States "first world"? Are you considered first class and we third class? Are you first rate and we third rate? Call us "developing countries." We are *not* a Third World country!'

"At that moment, I learned the value of using culturally appropriate language. Today, I cringe each time I hear the media or anyone else refer to developing countries as 'Third World.'

"Margie, when I came back to the United States, I was invited to tell my Cuban story at a local church. When I discussed the active role of the churches and staff at Matanzas Ecumenical Seminary since the 1959 Cuban Revolution, one of the men from the congregation who had served during the Korean conflict stood and angrily shouted, 'Sharon, you were there only *two weeks*. You know you were duped by the Cuban communists!' The pastor and elders of the church believed what I said was true, but I lost the majority of the audience once the 'communist' accusation was articulated. I was totally devastated!"

I continued to tell Margie my story. "That evening, I told Gary that I wished I had not gone to Cuba. To interact with women around the world on important issues was a major awakening for me. I had learned so much from the global women. However, knowing the truth was too difficult. I have that same feeling here in Nicaragua, Margie. When we learned about the literacy campaign, I thought about the Cuban experience and how good it was to have lived with Dora and Sergio, both committed educators and theologians. Why do we always equate the citizens of a country with their government? Tonight, I ponder these questions: Wouldn't it have been better for the United States to fund and equip the Nicaraguan Literacy Campaign instead of funding and equipping the contra war? Do the majority of American citizens understand what our government is doing to undermine Nicaragua? Do they know the truth?"

Margie had listened carefully and sympathetically to my story. She responded, "Sharon, the Reagan administration tries to justify the military buildup by claiming this small country of Nicaragua is a communist threat to the region. The US government blames the Sandinistas for their involvement with Cuba and the Soviet Union. That is one of their justifications for supporting the contras: to fight against communism. Nicaragua is not a communist country any more than your friend Dora is a communist."

She started to cry, then she told me a story. "One of the reasons I feel so strongly about our study group finding the truth in Nicaragua is that there are similarities here that mirror a current political violence, a civil war, taking place in El Salvador. El Salvador's military-led government is also supported by the United States.

"In 1980, my friend, Archbishop Oscar Romero, was assassinated in El Salvador, and Maryknoll Sisters Ida Ford, Maura Clark, and lay missionary Jean Donovan were raped and murdered by the Salvadoran military death squads. These friends were in El Salvador working with people of poverty. Archbishop Romero had called on the Carter administration to cut off US military aid to the Salvadoran government. When the US refused to cut off military aid, Archbishop Romero, in response to increased repression and death-squad killings, called upon members of the Salvadoran army and security forces to defy their orders and stop killing innocent people. Shortly following his pronouncement, Romero was assassinated while saying Mass in an El Salvadoran Catholic church."

She took a moment to calm her grief. "His murder happened one month after publicly asking the US government to stop military aid. My friends, Ida, Maura, and Jean were murdered a few months later. Since the 1979 Nicaraguan Revolution four years ago, no priests or nuns have been assassinated here; many work cooperatively with the Sandinista government. I have never seen religious liberty as ample in any country as I have experienced in Nicaragua."

She recited a piece of history from Thomas Jefferson: "We certainly cannot deny to other nations the principle whereon our government was founded, that every nation has the right to govern itself internally under what form it pleases."

"Sharon, the United States' policy of military intervention goes against the basic principles of our nation. The current military intervention in Nicaragua is as unjust as the US-backed, military-led government in El Salvador. This is the story we must tell when we arrive back in the United States.

"*If* we have no peace, it is because we have forgotten that we belong to each other."

—Mother Teresa

"We're Not Yet What We Want to Be, Neither What We Should Be, But We Give Thanks for Not Being What We Were."

After breakfast the following morning, Margie addressed our group. "I want to tell you what I've learned about Nicaragua's history from my former trips. Fifty thousand people were killed in a bitter civil war fought to end the injustices of the Somoza regime. The resistance activity culminated in the overthrow of Somoza on July 19, 1979. Somoza fled the country, leaving a huge national debt and operating funds that would last only three days. Somoza was a dictator supported by the United States. Under his forty-year leadership, the bulk of the population, particularly the 65 percent in rural Nicaragua, lived in abject poverty."

She continued. "Augusta Cesar Sandino was a poor peasant who organized resistance, in the 1920s, to US domination of Nicaragua. Sandino's national philosophy became the foundation for the revolution that challenged Somoza power. Sandino was assassinated in 1934 by the Somoza National Guard. Sandino is the namesake of the current Sandinista government; his spirit had emerged to form a new leadership. In 1961, the Sandinista National Liberation Front, founded by Carlos Fonseca—a Nicaraguan intellectual, an advocate for the poor, and considered 'the mind behind the revolution'—organized the struggle to return control of the country to the people. He brought together many groups—labor, students, women, peasants—and formed them into a common front named in honor of Sandino: the Sandinista Front for National Liberation (FSLN). Fonseca was killed in 1977 during the revolutionary war and, with Sandino, has become a national hero. Because both leaders were advocates for the poor, the 1979 revolution was considered the peasants' triumph after an unjust forty-year Somoza dictatorship."

Her voice rose in anger as she stomped around the room. "Somoza owned 8,260 square miles of land, while two-hundred thousand peasants were landless. Somoza cared only about the elite; he didn't give a damn about the majority of the population. The rich got richer, while the poor got poorer. Nicaragua, with its large lakes and coastal plain, was a playground for tourists, including US vacationers. The number one 'industry' for women under the Somoza regime was prostitution. Women were forced to sell their bodies for economic survival! You'll have an opportunity to meet some ex-prostitutes today." Distraught with anger, she sat to regain her composure.

Our study group sat in an uncomfortable silence for a few minutes. I wondered how each of us would react when meeting the ex-prostitutes. I knew this would be an extremely difficult day.

The nuns who would interpret for us and guide us through the meeting at the rehabilitation center gathered with us. They announced, "Today you'll have an opportunity to meet with Nicaraguan ex-prostitutes. They and their children reside in an educational building and housing center, where the women are learning new skills."

We traveled by bus to the rehabilitation center, located approximately forty kilometers from Managua. In the countryside, we saw a huge building that resembled a US college campus. Residence buildings, an education center, and grounds groomed with gardens surrounded the entire property. As we got closer, we saw two women standing on the porch at the entrance to the main building. They smiled and greeted us in Spanish as we walked up to the porch.

As we entered the front of the rehabilitation center, our study group stopped to read the entrance sign:

"We are not yet what we want to be,
neither what we should be,
but we give thanks for not being what we were."

Wiping tears from our eyes, we went inside to meet the ex-prostitutes.

The director of the rehabilitation center greeted us and invited us to meet each of the women studying there. As we walked around the large assembly room to greet each of the forty ex-prostitutes, they seemed eager and proud to show us their accomplishments. We followed them throughout the room as they showed us their beautifully crafted, brightly colored Nicaraguan artifacts, including wooden boxes and woven baskets. Also on display were crocheted, knitted, and sewed handicrafts the women had made. They were proud to tell us, through a translator, the detail involved in the work on each piece. They walked us through the adjoining library that was filled with books. My interpreter told me that reading had become a quality pastime for the women. "Books have provided the most beneficial results as the women work to recover from their former life of prostitution," she stated.

The women varied in ages from teenagers to late fifties. We gathered with them in a pleasant, sunlit room that provided space for their daily routine: learning, creating, reading, sewing, and conversing.

Sitting in a large circle with the women, the director told us of the former life of the prostitutes. "Under Somoza, prostitution was one way for women to feed their hungry and poverty-stricken families. Since the revolution, these women have changed dramatically: they learned new skills that have enhanced each of their lives. Typing, literacy, handicrafts, sewing, and tailoring, as well as cultural and political orientation, are all part of their education. When women leave the rehabilitation center, their education will enhance work opportunities in sewing factories, secretarial positions, office management, and educational facilities. They will be teachers of values for our young girls."

One of the married women explained, "This rehabilitation center also serves our husbands. They visit us once a week. The orientation here has enabled our husbands to understand the shame and rejection we wives felt as a direct result of the economic discrimination against us during the Somoza era. They are learning how we value our bodies, and how we want to be treated as human beings, not sexual objects. Some husbands, through rehabilitation with us, understand our pasts, knowing prostitution saved our families from starvation. We remain hopeful that our marriages will survive."

The rehabilitation center director responded, "We believe that the husbands who do not come for orientation during their wives rehabilitation will have a harder time when these women return to their homes. They will not understand their wives, who are now empowered and educated women."

A young mother in the circle started to sob. She looked at us as tears rolled down her beautiful face. "In order to feed our children, we were forced to sell our bodies as if we were merchandise. What mother could let her child starve to death?"

Everyone in the circle began to cry with her. The conversation made me realize how difficult life must have been for women in Nicaragua during the Somoza era. During the silence that followed her comment, I pondered the question: Why would the US government support a dictator who misused women, treating them as chattel property?

Breaking the silence, the women invited us to meet their families. We walked outdoors with them to see the facility that housed a daycare center and residence for their children. The children, from babies to eight years old, joined their mothers each evening to sleep at the rehabilitation residence. On the playground area, we saw young boys and girls playing joyfully on the swing sets, slides, and teeter-totters. Little girls sat on the concrete, playing jacks. Watching them made me think back to my easier Minnesota childhood, where we played jacks on the wooden floor of our one-room country schoolhouse.

The children smiled at us when our translators told them we had come from the United States to meet their mothers and see the education center. We gave them crayons along with a cultural coloring book. The staff of the center brought coffee, juice, and cookies for us to enjoy with the children and their mothers. While sitting at the picnic table, my translator told me that children ages six to eight attended class during the day from 8:00 AM to 3:30 PM, while their mothers were at the rehabilitation center. Children ages three to five had age-appropriate activities and lessons. The two year olds and younger were in a daycare housed within the residence building.

Following an hour outdoors enjoying a relaxing time with the mothers and children, we boarded our bus. The mothers and children waved as we departed. I reread the entrance sign. The last line, "but we give thanks for not being what we were," profoundly explained the rehabilitation story of these mothers, their children, and the center staff. I cried all the way back to our residence. The burden of knowing was beginning to devastate me! I kept grieving over the words of the young mother: "What mother could let her child starve to death?" On our trip back to Managua, none of us spoke; grief prohibited expression.

When we entered our room, Margie, eyes filled with tears, hugged me and, with a gentle voice, said, "What we experienced with the ex-prostitutes today is a profound reminder that the personal is political. Our personal lives and political lives are intrinsically connected. These newly empowered women are examples of living that reality daily.

"Sharon, I know that hearing the experiences of the ex-prostitutes was as difficult for you as it was for me. I have a gift for you, symbolic of our time with the women today. I hope it'll make you feel better." She bent down under her cot and pulled out a package she had purchased when our plane landed in Belize. She handed the package to me. "This is for you. You know it is uncharacteristic for me to shop, but I bought this gift because it reminded me of what I've watched happen to you as you've studied abroad, worked on important issues, and made informed decisions. I value our friendship and these four years we've worked together."

Happy with her kind gesture, I quickly opened the package. The gift was a beautiful, walnut statue of a woman. The statue was uniquely carved from one single piece of wood. Another, smaller feminine figure extended up over the top of the woman. Its form extended high beyond the woman's head, as if to soar freely in the air above her.

Margie looked at me quizzically then asked, "Do you know what this woman statue represents?"

"Margie, thank you! This is a magnificently carved statue. Isn't it a woman giving birth to her child? I can hardly wait to show my family!"

"Sharon, this statue—my gift to you for coming on the trip—represents a woman giving birth to *herself*. She is *you!*"

Twenty years older than me, Margie had gained much wisdom throughout her life. Now I understood why she had insisted I go on this study: as my mentor for the past four years, Margie expected me to follow in her footsteps. Forever, I would be committed to travel her challenging, revolutionary road toward peace with justice—no matter where the map would lead us, how difficult the journey, or how burdensome the reality of truth.

"If I can stop one heart from breaking, I shall not live in vain."

—Emily Dickinson

The Agrarian-Reform System

Thus far during our study, we had spent the majority of our time in Managua, the capital city. Within this small country of 2.4 million, 65 percent of the people lived in the rural areas. Our study agenda demanded we travel from the city to the countryside. To travel outside the city, we piled into open jeeps, excited to meet the people in Esteli, located approximately 120 kilometers north of Managua. Having lived on a farm during my early childhood, I was anxious to spend time with the farmers and learn about their newly developed agrarian-reform system.

The guides had informed us that since the revolution, land reform had been established in rural areas. One-third of the farmland, mainly idle lands formerly of the rich, had been given, free of charge, to poor peasants. Peasants now owned fifteen times more land than they had under Somoza. The peasants were allowed to have as much farmland as they could work. The government provided credit and technical assistance to the farmers for purchasing machinery, seed, farm supplies, and technical support from agricultural experts who were directing the agrarian-reform initiative. The Sandinistas would take over the land only if it was idle and didn't produce crops or if a farmer exploited the land by deteriorating the soil with chemicals. After the 1979 revolution, to enhance the agrarian-reform system, credit to small farms increased in *cordobas*, Nicaragua's monetary unit, by 800 percent.

Riding along country dirt roads, we passed miles of irrigated fields with a variety of planted crops and fruits. With few buildings on these huge sections of farmland, the planted fields reminded me of the corporate farming predominant in the United States. Our first stop was eight sections of land, a rural coffee plantation near the northern region of Nicaragua. The manager of the plantation stopped his work at the coffee-bean-sorting station. He greeted us with a smile and handed each of us an excellent cup of steaming, freshly brewed Nicaraguan coffee. We were delighted with his kind gesture. Three of the farmers stopped their laborious work to speak with us about their farming techniques. For the farmers' presentation—arranged by AMNLAE—we gathered around their workstation, where they were sorting coffee beans. One of the farmers, his forehead wet from labor in the hot sun, told us these facts:

"Like sugar and cotton, coffee is produced here for sale in the international market, so that dollars received can be used to repay the enormous debt incurred by Somoza. Coffee, as the main Nicaragua export crop, provides major economic development for our country. We also export cattle, cotton, sugar, and tobacco. Foods for consumption—corn, rice, and beans—are saved for use by our poorer population. The vital role of this agricultural production has made crops like coffee a key target of counterrevolutionary violence. If the contras can disrupt the coffee harvest, they can block the Sandinistas' attempts to get the economy working again."

He continued, "Since the revolution, moderate land-reform practices promoted the development of agricultural cooperatives. The government financially supported three thousand cooperative farms that include over a thousand acres each. We have eight hundred people on this plantation site when everyone is here harvesting coffee. Two hundred families live permanently at this location. Diesel fuel runs the coffee machine that takes husks off the beans after they have been washed. We are proud of the machinery that is adequate for our sustainable coffee production. The Soviet Union, through loans, helped us purchase tractors and farm equipment. This machinery has enhanced our coffee production and made our work less laborious."

I thought the tractors provided to the farmers by the Soviet Union were superior and more humane than the military equipment the United States provided the contra forces to burn the farmers' coffee harvest.

At this site, coffee bean sorting required no farm equipment; all work was manual labor. We stood and watched them as they carefully sorted then washed the coffee beans that had been stored in huge bins.

From a distance, we saw a woman carefully walk, step-by-step, down a steep mountain. She carried a large gunnysack of coffee beans over her shoulder. She came over to the coffee bean sorting station, dropped the heavy sack, spoke in Spanish to the plantation manager, than walked over to address our study group to tell us her story.

"In Nicaragua, the unions pay women the same amount as men. Before the revolution, we women worked, too, but only men were paid. Today, if our children help during harvest season, they are paid as well. Unions pay us about three times as much as when the Somoza family owned over half of the land."

Wiping sweat from her forehead, she continued. "Harvest season is once a year. Following harvest, we weed the fields, fertilize the land, and till the soil. During harvest, we worry constantly that workers will be ambushed and our coffee crops burnt by the contras. It is extremely dangerous at this location. Contras try to scare us from harvesting coffee, but we must continue. Our country's economy depends on coffee production.

Many of our friends and relatives have been killed and kidnapped at this plantation."

Her conversation with us recalled the comments at the memorial service about the youths ambushed and killed by the contras. I was appalled that these hard-working farmers were also threatened by violent contra attacks.

Two of the workers took us behind the coffee hacienda, the main gathering building on the plantation. Crude tunnels had been dug into the ground, where dirt surrounded the entry, sides, and floor. It reminded me of an animal's cave or a bear's hibernation den. The circumference and length was not large enough to accommodate more than nine adults at one time.

They explained, "This is where we hide when we fear contra air raids. A church bell rings to warn us of the danger. We have tunnels for our children, as well. Come over to the daycare center behind the church and we'll show you." As we walked to the daycare center, it was difficult for me to comprehend their daily routine: a constant fear of murder or the death of their innocent children and loved ones while working at the plantation.

We met the children at the farm-cooperative daycare. They were safe while their parents worked at the coffee plantation. We traveled through the underground tunnel in the basement of a large building that connected the daycare, dining room, and community center. The concrete tunnel protected children from contra attacks. The tunnel reminded me of the concrete bomb shelters built in backyards, home basements, and public buildings in the United States during the Cold War and McCarthy era. Would this tunnel protect Nicaraguans from contra air raids as the twelve-inch-thick bomb shelters were to protect us from "communist" nuclear radioactive dust?

As we walked across the street to the priest's home, I thought about what inhumane things we humans are capable of doing to one another. What awful hatred toward another human being could make these horrific inventions a reality?

The Catholic priest and his staff told us they were designated to ring the church bell whenever they heard or saw an indication of a contra attack. Contras would strike with air raids during the day and ambush with weapons at night. They invited us into their residence to see their photo display. "In this room, we have hung the pictures of our martyrs killed while protecting coffee crops." Around the large room, pictures of children, men, and women hung in eight-by-ten-inch frames. One group of pictures featured the youths we had seen in caskets at the memorial service.

At the coffee plantation, we gained a broader understanding of the damage and danger caused when contras burned the coffee crops to destabilize the Nicaraguan economy. For this community under strain, signs of fear, loss, and tension were evident everywhere. It was difficult to accept that the burden in their daily lives was caused by US military intervention in the country.

Enjoying Nicaraguan
Families in the Barrios

That evening, women in the country, members of AMNLAE, invited us to eat in their homes at Las Manos, near the Honduran-Nicaraguan Border. They wanted us to meet their families and show us their *casas* (homes) while we experienced Nicaraguan methods of cooking. In the backyard of each casa, stoves were fired up, cooking plantains, black beans, chicken, beef, tortillas, and rice.

Gathered among the children, men, and women, we experienced how Nicaraguan families lived. Extended families gathered around the table at mealtime. We ate, talked, laughed, and joined in the delight of the smiling mothers. They watched their children eat and enjoy with us the fabulous meal they'd cooked. *Mestizo*, a mixture of Spanish and Indian ethnic food, was tastefully delicious. I wanted to capture the love and spirit within these Nicaraguan families to take back home.

"Life is simple for us in the country," a mother told us. "We have found a new freedom since the revolution. We and our children are educated, our families have jobs, and if there is an event in the city, like the International Women's Day Celebration, the Sandinista government provides our transportation. We look forward to joining in celebration with you during International Women's Day."

That night, while sleeping in a home of one of the families, roosters crowed and goats wandered outside the door of the casa. I listened to the roosters and thought of my childhood. I told Margie, "Eating among the rural Nicaraguan families made me think of my rural growing-up years. Living in the country, families and neighbors truly cared for one another. Like our experience today, those were moments in time when the human condition was always the priority, over the maximization of profit. As a child, what I experienced on Hubbard Prairie in Minnesota was the collective energy, civility, and dignity of country folks."

Margie inquired, "Was it your childhood that helped you adapt so quickly to the simplicity of our life here?"

"Margie, from age three to fourteen, I lived on a 160-acre farm Dad inherited from my paternal Rezac grandparents. We had no running water, electricity, or indoor plumbing. Our farm abutted Palmer Lake; summers, we spent hours fishing and swimming. My father farmed, while my mother owned a boat-rental business that provided supplemental income for our family. The cold Minnesota winters were extremely difficult. By all standards, we were financially poor. But so were my country cousins, aunts, uncles, and farm families that lived around us.

"Our home became a gathering place for Mom's excellent homemade meals, joyful card games, dancing, dad's hair cutting, and quality conversations. With no telephone, neighbors stopped in anytime to visit. My parents were always prepared for company. I've never seen anyone work harder than my mom and dad yet have less materialistically. Today, eating among the Nicaraguan families recalled fond memories of why I loved growing up in the country during those formative childhood years."

Margie smiled, looked out at the barrios, and said, "Spending time today with the Nicaraguan families has been our best experience. It was refreshing to know that somewhere, within this cosmic weariness, the care and concern for the human condition is still a major priority."

As we left the homes of our Nicaraguan hosts the following morning, the country women in the barrios gathered and hugged each of us. They handed us their gift, a bag for lunch filled with *pupusas*—thick tortillas with beans. They waved as we climbed into our jeeps.

They continued to wave until the dust from the dirt road would no longer let us view their smiling faces and white-as-snow, starched aprons. I could envision my beautiful, green-eyed mother in her white, starched apron standing there smiling and waving among them.

The experience in the country added more fodder for thought. The farmers and women in the barrios were experiencing better lives since the revolution as a result of the cooperative efforts by the Sandinista government. The major obstacle that hindered their life was the threat of the contra attacks, supported by US tax dollars. The vision of truth was becoming clear.

"*H*alf the misery in the world comes of want of courage to speak and bear the truth plainly."

—Harriet Beecher Stowe

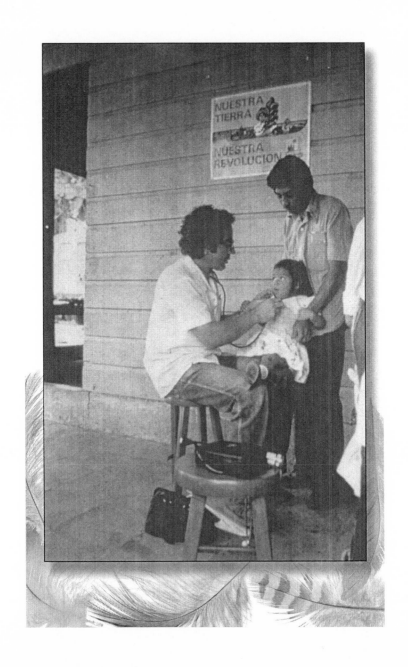

Visiting the Children's Hospital

Back in Managua, we stopped to discuss the national system of healthcare with the director of Nicaragua's first children's hospital, Dr. Emundo Miranda. He greeted us then took us on a tour of the facility. He was proud to show us their state-of-the-art, extremely clean clinic adjacent to the hospital. In the hospital conference room, Dr. Miranda told us about the advancements in healthcare since the revolution.

"Last month, a massive health campaign was begun to train thousands of health workers to carry out vaccination programs, teach basic sanitation, and provide preventative healthcare in villages throughout Nicaragua. In Nicaragua, healthcare is based on two principles: first, that all the people have a right to good healthcare; and second, that the government must do all it can to provide quality healthcare."

He told about their health statistics. "We are proud of our advances in healthcare. Since 1979, the infant death rate, a good indicator of the overall health of a country, has declined from 120 per 1,000 births to 88 per 1,000 births."

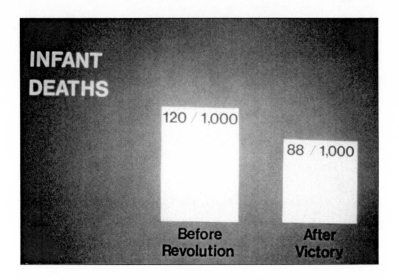

He continued. "The number of clinics has increased from 29 to 150. Most clinics are located in rural areas. All are free. Improved healthcare is most apparent in rural Nicaragua, where medical facilities did not exist during the Somoza era. Immunizations have more than tripled. We had 120 cases of measles last year. Prior to the revolution, there were three thousand cases. A decrease in outbreaks of typhoid and measles, with a virtual end to the misery of polio, are major healthcare advancements."

He proudly announced, "Our Sandinista government's emphasis on low-cost healthcare has made these statistics possible. The United Nations Children's Fund, UNICEF, described our advancements as 'one of the most dramatic improvements in child survival in the developing world.'"

Margie asked, "What surgeries do you perform in the country?"

"Currently, open-heart surgery is too serious to do here, as are transplants. We have neither the expertise nor the equipment. We depend on international hospitals for major surgeries. We invested heavily in this children's hospital to provide quality healthcare to 45 percent of the Nicaraguan population. Due to war casualties, currently, 45 percent of the Nicaraguan population is under fifteen years of age."

I asked, "What is the average salary of a doctor?"

"All doctors earn an equal salary of ten thousand dollars maximum, an adequate income to live comfortably with our low cost of living. They work eight hours a day. Doctors spend five years in medical school and two years of internship at a hospital. Most of our doctors want to work in public hospitals. Fifteen to twenty percent of the former doctors left the country, fearing the revolution. Some have returned, but we have a shortage. There are seven hundred doctors enrolled in our Nicaraguan medical school. At this rate, with our current population, we should have a sufficient number of medical doctors to sustain our healthcare needs in the future. Particular effort is being made to provide health services in rural areas. Prior to the revolution, the rural area, especially the poor, had been totally neglected."

He smiled and then, with pride, stated, "Because of the belief that health is the right of the people, a goal has been established to provide national healthcare through hospitals with a backup system at health centers. I am certain we will meet that goal."

That evening, back at our residence, our study group discussed the advantages of a national healthcare program and the advances the Sandinista government had provided the Nicaraguan population since the revolution. We agreed that healthcare is a right for all persons. We questioned if adequate healthcare for all could ever become a reality within the United States.

Following our discussion, Margie stated, "I'm happy that AMNLAE provided our visit to the children's hospital. I believe our country needs to come up with an American solution to reform the American healthcare system. What a benefit national healthcare would be for the marginalized people of our country! Without question, adequate healthcare is an equitable right for all humankind."

"Caution, careful people always casting about to preserve their reputation or social standards never can bring about reform. Those who are really in earnest are willing to be anything or nothing in the world's estimation, and publically and privately, in season and out, avow the sympathies with despised ideas, and bear the consequences."

—Susan B. Anthony

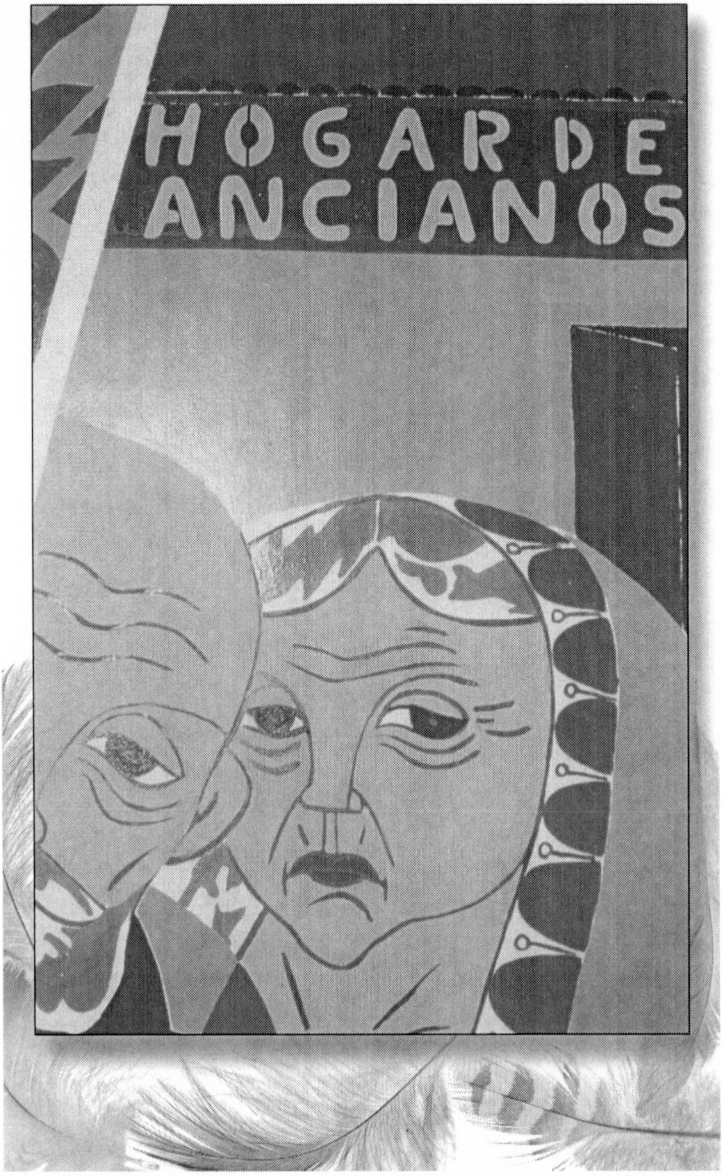
HOGAR DE
ANCIANOS

Celebrating Life with
Nicaraguan Senior Citizens

The following day, our guides informed us that AMNLAE had provided us an opportunity to travel to the Nicaraguan Senior Center, twenty kilometers outside of Managua. When we arrived, we saw murals depicting happy faces painted on the entrance to the senior center, a large building that resembled a one-story motel. The grounds surrounding the building were adorned with beautiful, green perennials and a variety of colorful flowers.

Seniors met us at the door and welcomed us to their "home away from home." A group of them took our study group and translators on a tour of their facility. They were extremely proud of their library, filled with books; their gardens they helped plant and maintain; their swimming pool, used for exercise; and their sunlit room inside, that offered special moments for conversation. Following the tour, the center director invited us to join the seniors in the dining room. "We want you to understand the lives of Nicaraguan seniors since the revolution," she stated. Following our meal, they told us their life stories.

One of the women stated, "We are a happy and appreciative group of seniors. Our lives have changed since the revolution. Before, we had no place to congregate. Most of the time, we just sat in our casas; now, we are brought to our charming clubhouse by bus to enjoy days filled with conversation in the community room, relaxation at the swimming pool, or reading in the library. We also play a variety of games, create crafts, or tend the beautiful flower gardens. Because of the quality of our lives today, we named the 1979 revolution, 'the Triumph'!"

One of the men entertained us with recorded Nicaraguan music. As the calypso-style music continued, a senior stood and asked, "Would any of you like to dance?" I volunteered, but I had a difficult time keeping up to his fast-moving feet. With patience, my partner continued to try to teach me the dance and help my feet move as quickly as his. One of the women at the senior center asked a senior in our study group to join her. Alongside us, the two of them looked more impressive than the attempts I had made dancing with my partner. The seniors invited all of us to take a dance lesson. We all agreed to try dancing Nicaraguan style. They patiently led us in what reminded me of a combination of the cha-cha and rumba. Their movements were swift and delightfully rhythmic. They reminded me of my parents' unique style when they polkaed so beautifully around a dance floor. Like the polka in my childhood, this swift dance required a rhythm difficult for most of us in the study group to master.

After four hours with the seniors, we said our farewells and thanked them for a fabulous day. In response, one woman smiled, stood, then proudly announced to us, "Within my lifetime, these are the best days that I've had the opportunity to live."

That evening, Margie remarked, "That's the lifestyle *I* want to live in my aging years. I think I'll come back here and join the Nicaraguan seniors. Did you see their fabulous library?" I assured her that I had. However I knew my limited Spanish proficiency wouldn't afford me the pleasure of reading books there, as it would Margie, who had studied the language.

As Margie and I were preparing for sleep, one of the US Catholic sisters in our study group, Sister Betty, came into our room. We could tell from her expression that she was distraught; then she broke down into tears. Margie embraced her and invited her to sit with us.

After composing herself, she exclaimed, "I must talk to you! I came on this study tour to learn the truth, but now I am so ashamed of our country! The best way for us to deal with our study here and commitment to the people is to try to influence our own government back home. We must continue to deepen our knowledge and not feel guilty about something we did not understand before. But now we know! In order to get rid of anger, we must do something. Watching the seniors today, I know how I want to motivate my life. As a woman of faith, I am committed to taking on the sins of my country."

I felt exactly as Sr. Betty did; I knew we had a major responsibility to tell the truth when we returned home. Margie reminded Sr. Betty about the murders of their friends.

"Remember when our friends Ida, Maura, Jean, and Archbishop Romero were murdered in El Salvador? Because of the tragic deaths of these beloved friends, I went there to find the investigative facts of their murders and determine the conflict taking place between the El Salvadoran, military-led government and the Far-abundo Marti National Liberation Front. There, as in post-revolution Nicaragua, economic and political tensions were on the rise, fueled by the widening gap between the extremely rich and extremely poor. Tension and violence in El Salvador caused the outbreak of the current civil war there."

She continued as Betty and I listened. "The desire to prevent the kind of 'leftist takeover' in Cuba and Nicaragua motivated the United States to get militar-ily involved in El Salvador. After our friends were murdered in 1980 and two American land-reform advisers were gunned down in El Salvador in 1981, the US Congress subsequently decided to dissolve aid, only as improvements in the Salvadoran human-rights situation became evident and the investigations of the murders were revealed. Military aid was cut off only briefly, pending the investigation of these murders. To date, that investigation has not been clarified, but in El Salvador, as in Nicaragua, the Reagan administration views the El Salvador military as a potential barrier against communism, therefore military funding has been continued. Both the El Salvadoran military and the Nicaraguan contras are violators of human rights."

Sister Betty responded, "When we return to the United States, I will do whatever it takes to change the current US policy that provides funding for the contras.

As a woman of faith, I believe God, who lives at the juncture of justice, demands that of me!"

When Sister Betty left, Margie and I knew her life had changed forever.

The Rehabilitation Center for Ex-Somoza National Guard

"*Today, we will meet* with the interns at the La Granja prison farm, located thirty kilometers from Managua," our guides announced. "This is the farm where ex-Somoza National Guard, the country's elite torturing squad, served prison sentences. After being rehabilitated, the interns have developed new skills and values while they have learned to manage the productive farm. Twelve men chose to live onsite to maintain the buildings, plant and harvest the crops, and take care of the cattle. We've been here before. You need not be concerned. The rehabilitated men who reside here are friendly and kind."

As our bus pulled up to the main building, we saw no fences surrounding the property; the farm looked more like an agricultural campus than a prison farm. An ex-Somoza National Guardsman welcomed us. Our study group and interpreters stood outside the farm site as he told us their story. "We installed and built everything that is here. The running water, paved floor, and homes were all work accomplished by us. Agriculture is our major labor, but we also do carpentry, plumbing, and mechanics. We grow tomatoes, watermelon, corn—all foods for consumption. Half of the crops are given to our families, and the remainder we take to market. What profit we make at the market, we invest in additional crops."

He continued. "In the beginning, there were six thousand Somoza National Guardsmen here with us; another five thousand fled to Honduras. Of the six thousand of us formerly here, all have met the government's expectations to live nonviolently within the Nicaraguan society. They have all served their sentences and are reunited with their families. None have had to return. Many are working in governmental reconstruction projects to help rebuild our country's infrastructure, and some continue to farm. The major requirements at this farm are good behavior and a quality work ethic. There are twelve of us living here now. We farm while tending the ten cows and fourteen calves that were donated by the government."

One of the other men joined in. "From the beginning, there were no fences or armed guards. Only one person escaped, prompted by his mental illness. We felt we could not disappoint the Sandinista government, who had given us this freedom and rehabilitation opportunity. That is why our rehabilitation here has been 100 percent successful: we trust the Sandinista government as they trusted us."

We watched the men as they stood outside and finished their chores. A sign on the fence read: "Hatred only begets more hatred. The past is the past. Let us now speak of the future."

We thanked the men for their time during their busy farm season and our opportunity to spend over an hour there. As we left the rehabilitation center on our trip back to Managua, one of our guides explained, "If all the ex-Somoza National Guard had come to this farm, Nicaragua wouldn't be experiencing a civil war. The contras are a remnant of this group, but instead of working at this rehabilitation farm, they continue Somoza tactics. Currently, they live along the Honduran border.

"Many of the contras are young boys from poor families, surviving without much food. The majority are illiterate. They are lured by the ex-Somoza National Guard with the offer of meat, cruises, television sets, and trips to the United States' Fort Bragg 'military academy.' They are led to believe they're fighting against communists who will take everything away from them. We think mind-controlling drugs may explain their horrible crimes of rape, beheadings, and torture. They'll kill anyone who supported the revolution or the Sandinista government."

Our study group was shocked that the US administration was so ill informed about the realities taking place in Nicaragua. This rehabilitation farm was an example of how a quality, humane life can be restored to people who previously used inhumane tactics.

I thought life in the mountainous countryside had seemed so simple. But people in the country had been faced with threats by those wanting to topple the Nicaraguan government. After visiting the rehabilitation farm, a member of our study group questioned, "Why do the contras continue to kill innocent coffee pickers?

Why do they rape, behead, and torture people? How can the United States fund this violent terrorism?"

Over dinner, we discussed the rehabilitation prison farm. Each of us agreed with their philosophy, "Hatred only begets more hatred." We had witnessed the violent hatred the contras exhibited daily in Nicaragua.

Later in the evening, when we got to our room, I asked Margie, "Why do you think the United States encourages this horrible behavior by providing military aid and training young contras in methods of torture?"

"That is what we're here to determine, Sharon. This is not the first time our country's fear of communism supported an unjustifiable war. This contra war is similar to the Vietnam War. Because Cubans aided the Nicaraguan literacy campaign and the Soviet Union sold them tractors and gave them loans, Nicaraguan Sandinistas are labeled 'communists' by our government.

"US-sponsored terrorism against Nicaragua has been condemned by the United Nations, the World Court, and key US allies including England, France, Italy, Japan, Mexico, and Brazil. Polls show most Americans oppose US efforts to overthrow the Nicaraguan government.

"The United States blames Nicaragua for not holding elections in the three years since the 1979 revolution. It took the United States *eight* years following *our* revolution to hold elections. This is a true, historical fact: people throughout the world could get along if their governments would not intervene.

"The Sandinistas are committed to helping the poor, who have suffered for so many years under Somoza. Sandinistas are seeking what is best for all Nicaraguans, regardless of their socioeconomic status. You and I have witnessed daily the Nicaraguan people striving to create a new reality of economics and politics—a reality that is neither Cuban nor Russian, but does not see in the US government a model to be copied, either."

I agreed with Margie's perspective. Pondering her answer, I sat in silence. She went over to her cot, sat, and stared out the window. After a few moments, with a contemplative look on her face, she addressed me with these words: "Sharon, promise me, if I die, you'll make certain that my ashes come back here to get interred in the barrio of Managua. This is where I witness good news to the poor and an ongoing revolution that demands justice, as well as a majority of people who work against injustice."

I heard her message, but I couldn't answer. Her request made me speechless. Lying on my cot a few feet from her, I thought, *What if Margie dies? What will I do without her in my life?* I covered my head with a pillow to quiet my sobbing.

Visiting the Folk-Art Capital
or Hellish War Zone

*H*aving *traveled extensively throughout* the country, we had only four more days to complete our study in Nicaragua. It was early morning when the four nuns came to our room. One of the nuns asked Margie if we wanted to travel to the Honduran border. "At the border, you'll gain additional knowledge about the war. The experience at the war zone will help concretize your story once you return home."

Margie looked at me. "Sharon, will you go? Because of the danger lurking in the mountains and landmines along the way, I certainly cannot expect our entire study group to take this trip. At breakfast, I'll determine how many want to travel with us."

"*Us* must mean I *am* going, Margie. Is this when you're going to put your body over mine when the bullet comes?"

She smiled, nodded her head up and down, and said, "Yes!"

At breakfast, Margie stood and addressed our study group. Even without wearing a turban wrapped around

77

her head, her tall, huge, robust demeanor reminded me of Sojourner Truth. I halfway waited for Margie to deliver Sojourner's famous, "Ain't I a Woman" speech.

She began. "Today, we have one more fabulous educational opportunity. Our guides informed me this morning that we can travel again to the countryside, this time on the Pan-American Highway. We will go to the Honduran border, the hellish war zone where so many atrocities have taken place. Because of the dangerous landmines and possible contra raids along the route, this trip is not a mandatory part of our study. Please do not feel obligated to travel with us. Our trip will take the entire day. How many of you want to go?"

Slowly, fifteen hands went up; mine was one of them. A broad smile filled Margie's entire face; her green, Irish eyes sparkled like lit birthday candles. I could tell she was extremely pleased.

Our guides told the other women in our study group, "You who will not be traveling with us to the border can visit the town of Masaya, the folk-art capital of Nicaragua. Nicaraguans have developed culture as a means of shaping the new society. Culture is the artistic arm of the revolution. You have seen examples of the arts and crafts that flourish throughout the country on billboards and in buildings. You'll enjoy meeting our Maryknoll poet-priest friend, Ernesto Cardenal. Ernesto is Nicaragua's minister of culture."

I love folk art and would have enjoyed visiting the folk art capital, but I knew it was too late to change my mind. I could not disappoint Margie; however, the folk-art capital of Nicaragua sounded more inviting and safer to me than the dangerous war zone from hell along the Nicaraguan-Honduran border.

Traveling to the War Zone

*A*s *we got ready* to leave for the border by 8 a.m. the guides announced that AMNLAE had provided an opportunity for us to stop for lunch at a tobacco site. Seventeen of us, plus our four guides, piled into three jeeps. We were packed so tightly together we felt like canned sardines. I occupied a rear seat by the bumper in jeep number one. Margie sat up front in the passenger seat.

We traveled two hundred kilometers to Jalapa, near the Honduran-Nicaraguan border, and stopped at the cooperative tobacco warehouse around noon. The workers greeted us and invited our group to join them for lunch. After we had eaten tortillas, plantains, and beans, the workers proudly showed us their new facility. The warehouse that stored the tobacco looked like a downsized silo, but instead of smelling like corn fodder, it smelled like a pipe that had been smoked with cherry tobacco.

At the warehouse, the manager explained, "Tobacco, another export crop, provides additional economic development for the country. Each dollar helps us with the enormous financial drain caused by the undeclared war funded by the United States."

We were aware that their lives experienced constant danger when they worked this close to the Honduran-Nicaraguan border. A young female worker at the tobacco warehouse told us about the death of her mother, father, and sister when the contras attacked the village of Jalapa in December 1982. Now, at age sixteen, she had to care for her three younger siblings.

She invited us to look behind the tobacco warehouse. She and two of the workers showed us hand-dug trenches, similar to what we had seen at the coffee hacienda. Both the women and the men utilized the trenches while guarding their cooperative. We also saw a crudely dug hole where a child or two could crawl in for protection from air raids.

When we left for the border after hearing of the

dangers that these kind, hardworking people faced each day, our group was more anxious about our trip.

As we came closer to the Honduran-Nicaraguan border, we passed two truckloads of young Sandinista soldiers on the road. They waved to us. The nun in our jeep told us, "These soldiers are going for their night duty to protect the coffee crops. At night is when the enemy usually strikes! That's why we must leave the border before dark."

Margie turned around and reiterated her statement to me. "Sharon, if the bullet comes, remember I'll place my body over yours." Her comment didn't make me feel more secure. I knew the others in our jeep were equally scared.

As we crossed the bridge that the nuns told us replaced one our government had blown up a few months earlier, my interpreter explained to me, "The Sandinista guards were at the Honduran-Nicaraguan border each night to watch for contra invaders. We are traveling to the location where the youths, whose memorial service we attended, had been massacred."

After riding twenty kilometers, we stopped our jeeps at the Honduran-Nicaraguan border. With no buildings or military trucks to obstruct our view, the golden, mountainous landscape in the background made the location appear magnificently beautiful and peaceful. Young Honduran military guards armed with rifles stood in a row along their border. They were only a few feet across the white line that indicated where one country ended and the other began. The white line was the only visible sign that divided the two countries in this "peaceful appearing" war zone. As the soldiers watched us, I wondered if these young Honduran men understood the root causes of the conflict. Were they aware of the tragedies that had taken place in the region?

Margie went to the border of the two countries and knelt there in silent prayer. As she straddled the white line along the border, the rest of our study group and interpreters joined her. With the young soldiers looking on, rifles in hand, none of us felt frightened. I'd never prayed so earnestly for peace.

After the prayer, we walked over to the Nicaraguan side of the border. I saw a young teenager standing on patrol. He was armed with a rifle and wore military fatigues. He looked about the age of my fifteen-year-old son, Mark. I walked up to salute him then said, "I have a son in high school about your age."

His dark eyes looked directly at me, and he smiled.

"My name is Jorge," he said in English, then he stated, "I wish I could trade this rifle and war zone for a pen and pencil in school."

He pointed to the coffee field to show me where his friends had been ambushed and killed while protecting coffee crops. Our study group walked through the burnt rubble of ashes and smelled the ashen, charred earth beneath our feet. The stench and surrounding environment reminded me of the concentration camps I had toured in Dachau while studying the Jewish Holocaust.

As I walked along the perimeter of the charred field, I noticed a round, shiny piece of brass. I picked it up; it was a used bullet. I turned it around in my hand and looked at the insignia on the metal casing; "USA" was clearly engraved on it. No, not my country!

Mortified, I realized that this used bullet provided proof; it validated what we had learned at the memorial service. Yes, the contras were militarily armed by the United States! I shoved the bullet into my pocket. I could hardly wait to show Margie.

It was late afternoon when we left for Managua and the sky was beginning to darken. The guides, aware that we had stayed too long, suggested a different route back. As we traveled along unpaved roads through the rugged mountains of the northern region, we were tense and anxious. We wondered when the violent contras would strike again. Would *we* be their massacred victims this time?

For the first time since we landed in Nicaragua, I was trembling from fright as we traveled back along the winding, dusty dirt roads. Riding in the rear seat of the bumpy jeep, I looked at the back of Margie's head that bobbed up and down directly in front of me. I wanted to yell, "Hey Margie, how in the hell are you going to get back here when the 'Made in the USA' bullet comes toward me?" The mood in our jeep was somber; I knew my friends were frightened, too.

After what felt like an eternity in Hades during the longer route back, we finally arrived at our Managua living quarters at 8:30 PM. Drained from the long day and covered in dust from the open-air jeeps, we went directly to our rooms, avoiding the evening meal and conversations with the other group. We didn't want to hear about their unique and glorious experience at the Masaya Folk Art Center.

As Margie and I entered our room, I pulled the bullet out of my pocket. "Look what I found under the ashes in the burnt coffee field."

Margie put on her reading glasses and carefully examined the bullet. She rolled it around in both hands. When she saw "USA" on the metal casing, she exclaimed, "Sharon, this is a fantastic find! We can take this used bullet home as additional proof that the United States has armed the contra death squads!" I felt proud of my discovery and could hardly wait to show others this profound piece of evidence.

Neither of us cared about the dust that covered every inch of our bodies. Exhausted, we collapsed onto our cots. I tucked the used bullet securely under my pillow.

"It isn't enough to talk about peace. One must believe in it. And it isn't enough to believe in it. One must work at it."

—Eleonor Roosevelt

Celebrating International Women's Day

During breakfast, we discussed the trip to the Nicaragua-Honduran border with the rest of our study group, who was astounded by our experience and the bullet as evidence of US military support to the contras. They told us that their experience at the art center had proven that art was an integral part of the revolutionary culture.

With only three days left in Nicaragua, all of us were excited to celebrate International Women's Day. International Women's Day, March 8, had been declared a national holiday in Nicaragua. Women came to Managua from all over the country to participate in the conference that celebrated their achievements. We looked forward to being reunited with women whom we had met in various locations throughout the countryside. We knew the mothers of the heroes and martyrs would be in attendance at this annual event.

On behalf of Church Women United and our study group, Margie, as one of the speakers, was prepared to give her presentation that followed a speech by AMNLAE director Doris Tijerino. Margie told us she would thank

AMNLAE, sponsors of International Women's Day, for hosting our study group, providing the lodging and transportation. She would also recognize our guides as our excellent interpreters and thank them for their constant travel and work on our behalf. In solidarity with women around the world, this was to be our one day of relaxation and celebration while in Nicaragua.

We gathered with the huge crowd outside AMNLAE Headquarters. Chairs were set up on the lawn in front of the podium. The mothers who had lost daughters and sons to war were seated in the front row. Our study group sat together in a designated area behind the mothers. We recognized the women with whom we had shed tears at the memorial service. Each of us felt a need to apologize to them. We knew Margie would offer consoling words on our behalf during her speech.

Doris Tijerino, president of AMNLAE, welcomed the crowd in Spanish. I was grateful she allowed time for our interpreters to translate each word. Doris stated, "We are delighted you are here to celebrate the seventieth anniversary of International Women's Day! This day is also commemorated at the United Nations and is designated in many countries as a national holiday."

She continued. "During International Women's Day, women on all continents—often divided by national boundaries and by ethnic, linguistic, cultural, economic, and political differences—gather together to celebrate our day. This is a time for reflection, when we look back to a tradition that represents at least seven decades of women's struggles for equality, peace with justice, and development."

She looked at the mothers in the front row. "We Nicaraguan women have lived that struggle. Before the revolution, we were considered nothing but chattel property by Somoza. During the revolution, we were aware that we had to take up arms along with the men to fight against the Somoza regime. If we did not participate militarily, how could we expect to be equal to the men in our country?"

She smiled at our study group. "Today, we welcome and thank our American sisters who have traveled and studied from city to countryside. They have come here to gain an understanding of our lives prior to and since the revolution. US sisters, I want to tell you my story. It is the story of so many women's lives in our country. The vivid red scars on my face show you the torture of violent actions by the Somoza National Guard. I have been raped, tortured, and widowed twice. The last time, they beat me then stuck a gun up my vagina and left me for dead. But I survived!" Tears filled the eyes of our study group and interpreters.

She paused a few moments then added, "During the resistance, our Sandinista minister of interior, Tomas Borge, was also tortured, while his wife was brutally murdered. After the revolution, Borge stated that his personal vengeance toward the Somoza National Guard would be to provide schools and flowers for their children. We do not want to continue the anger, torture, and killings. Since the revolution, we have worked unceasingly for peace with justice. We need your help! When you go home, tell the truth about what you have seen and experienced while in our country. We beg of you, make your government stop providing aid and military equipment to the contra death squads!"

The crowd erupted in harmonious chanting: "Sandino lives in the fight for peace! Sandino lives in the fight for peace!" We US women joined them in their chant: "Sandino lives in the fight for peace!"

When the crowd quieted, Doris introduced Margie. "I am honored to introduce Sister Margie Tuite. Sister Margie has traveled to our country numerous times. Throughout her lifetime, she has constantly worked for justice. Margie is a leading voice in demanding an equal role for women in the Roman Catholic Church, an advocate for the poor, and an educator on a broad range of social-justice issues. She's had a major role in the US civil rights, peace, and women's movements. She has never stopped making the connections between sexism, racism, militarism, nationalism, and all forms of violence."

Doris continued praising Margie. "Sister Margie opposes ageism, classism, ethnocentrism, homophobia, racism, sexism, and war. She has witnessed the contras' destruction of Nicaragua's agriculture cooperatives and has studied our advancements since the revolution. We women of Nicaragua love you, Sister Margie. You are truly our advocate and hero!"

Margie stood, flashed her delightful smile, and addressed the crowd. "Thank you, Doris! I am humbled by your kind words. Women of Nicaragua, you are my heroes and martyrs. You have remained in a humanitarian struggle that demands peace with justice. During our study, we have witnessed your excellent work and advancements throughout the entire country.

"We are grateful to AMNLAE for hosting us and providing our transportation while in your country, and to my four Catholic sisters who have been our guides and translators at each event. You have offered us an experience of a lifetime. In no way do we claim to be experts after a brief two weeks of study; yet, as we journeyed throughout your country, from early morning to late evening, it became apparent that the revolutionary process could be successful—if not undermined by the United States funding and militarily arming the contras.

"We are committed to return to our country to tell your story. All women in our study group will work to demand our government change its current policy toward Nicaragua.

"We will educate our families, friends and professional colleagues by organizing study groups, focus sessions, and assemblies.

"We will show our pictures, videos, slides, and literature as proof of our experience.

"We will write our congressional representatives and contact our local media to inform them that we oppose US military intervention in your country—and explain the reasons why.

"We will contact the Reagan administration and demand, 'No more military aid to the contras!'

"We will join with other peace groups, and I personally will pledge to do an act of civil disobedience with my colleagues who also oppose US military intervention in Nicaragua.

"Last year, I founded the Women's Coalition to Stop US Intervention in Central America and the Caribbean. I believe that between women, there are no boundaries. The coalition, as a human-rights group, is committed to stopping all US support to the contras and other violent groups, ending the embargo and restoring full diplomatic and trade relations with your country, and requesting our country supply economic aid only to governments like yours, who have shown a commitment to raise the living standards of the poor.

"Mothers of the heroes and martyrs, we honor you today. As women from the United States, we sincerely apologize that our government has caused the deaths of your heroic youth. We join with you in solidarity, and we pledge, on this International Women's Day, that no issue of a woman's womb will be destroyed again on the battlefield of human strife. As mothers of the martyrs, you have paid the ultimate price. We are extremely sorry for your sacrifice."

Tears flowed from our eyes and the eyes of everyone

around us; emotion was evident in the mothers and martyrs sitting in front of us.

"We promise you that we'll go back to the United States and tell our collective stories. We know your struggle for self-determination, for political and economic survival, is centered in the call for freedom and human dignity. I will be back in the future to join you. United, we will work for social and economic justice. Women of Nicaragua, you offer us hope for the creation of a better, more humane world."

When Margie finished speaking, the crowd gave her a standing ovation. In the front row, a mother of the heroes and martyrs continued to stand afterward, while tears rolled down her face. She looked at our study group sternly then faced the crowd and pleaded with us: "Tell your people that we want the same things you do. We want peace and a chance for our children to grow up healthy, go to school, and get decent jobs. We are a small, poor country. We cannot hurt you. Please stop hurting us!"

Our study group stood and gave her an ovation, hoping to show that we heard her plea. The crowd once again erupted in harmonious chants of "Sandino lives in the fight for peace! Sandino lives in the fight for peace!" The chanting continued as we walked to the reception that followed.

All who were present to celebrate International Women's Day attended the reception held at the AMNLAE Headquarters. We sipped fresh pineapple juice and enjoyed the lunch prepared by AMNLAE. During lunch, the AMNLAE legal advisor sitting at our table told our study group that an early victory for women was the prohibition of the publication and distribution of images that used women as sexual objects for promotional purposes. She stated, "Recently, the government passed a 'Law on Nurture,' which includes the stipulation that men have an obligation to share in the upbringing of their children. This law relieves women of some of the unequal burden for those who had to formerly bear this responsibility by themselves."

After telling us examples of the equality they were trying to achieve, she turned to me and asked, "Why hasn't the Equal Rights Amendment been ratified in the United States?"

What could I say that wouldn't sound trite, after all that the Nicaraguan women had accomplished in just three years?

"*L*aws will not eliminate prejudice from the hearts of human beings. But there is no reason to allow prejudice to continue to be enshrined in our laws to perpetuate injustice."

—Shirley Chisholm

The Pope's Visit

During our study, we were aware that Pope John Paul II was scheduled to make a pastoral visit in Managua. In the past ten days, everywhere we went, from cities to the countryside, signs were displayed in preparation for the Pope's Mass. Pictures were in windows, on signboards, and on walls and posters. Anyone who could afford money for a newspaper studied a map that detailed the route from his former engagement in Leon, two hundred kilometers north of Managua. Nicaraguans wanted to know where they could board a free bus to the July 19 Revolutionary Plaza.

The Sandinista government used rationed gasoline so that people from the most remote areas of Nicaragua could attend. In the early morning on the day of the Pope's visit, streams of buses, loaded with passengers left the countryside to see the Pope in Managua. The day was declared a national holiday. The Catholic sisters invited Margie and the other nuns who were members of our study group to go by van to the July 19 Revolutionary Plaza; they were invited to sit on the platform next to the Pope. The rest of us were asked to gather among the crowds at the event later. We were curious about the Mass, hoping that the Pope would feel the excitement of the people gathered and address the mothers and fathers who had lost their children to war.

Margie told us she was reluctant to go with her friends and be stationed as a guest of honor on the platform that was staged outdoors where the Pope would speak. "The undeclared contra war has created a period of polarization between the Nicaragua Catholic hierarchy and Nicaraguan Catholics," she informed us. "There are also tensions between the Catholic hierarchy and the Sandinista state. I know the Pope is opposed to Liberation Theology, taught by my Maryknoll friends in Nicaragua's Christian-based communities, because it is a political theology that interprets the teachings of Jesus Christ in terms of being liberated from unjust economic, political, or social conditions. Within Nicaragua, Liberation Theology has empowered and educated the majority. It has enhanced their Christian faith, not destroyed it. I fear the pontiff will discredit Liberation Theology, the Maryknoll nuns, the Jesuit priests, and the entire revolution. Vatican II addressed the relations between the Roman Catholic Church and the modern world. I'm not convinced Pope John Paul II embraces the Vatican II accomplishments established by his predecessors Pope John XXIII and Pope Paul VI."

The nuns pleaded with Margie. "You must come and sit in solidarity with us! We need your support on the platform!" At noon, two hours prior to the Pope's scheduled arrival, Margie reluctantly left with them early enough to be seated on the platform. She was extremely concerned about what the Pope's message would entail. I knew her concern about the Catholic Church hierarchy. The Pope, archbishops, and bishops had expressed opposition to women's ordination, a position she and her friends supported. Margie always challenged the patriarchal demands of the church that she felt placed women in submissive roles. I agreed with her that women should be ordained and struggled also with the patriarchy embraced by the Vatican. I was concerned that she felt obligated to be seated on the platform instead of attending the event with us, as she wanted.

Our study group planned to ride to the plaza as soon as the van Margie and the nuns left in returned. However, when we realized the van was not coming back for us, we set out on foot. By the time we had walked four blocks and joined the mass of humanity that converged on the main highway to the plaza, it was apparent why the van hadn't returned: with the huge amount of people walking to the plaza, vehicular traffic couldn't travel on the road.

We walked four miles and joined a happy and colorful crowd. Bright umbrellas gave protection from the hot sun. Most of the pedestrians were carrying flags: yellow and white for the Pope; blue and white for the nation; red and black for the Sandinista Revolution. Near the plaza, we could hear announcements that pleaded with the crowd to stay back from the platform, so that persons who had fainted from the heat could be carried out safely. I worried about Margie: Would she be overcome with heat? Would she be safe? Would her support for women's ordination, or her work with the

Maryknoll nuns and Jesuit priests, be compromised by the Pope's message?

Around two o'clock, the time of the Pope's scheduled arrival, our group decided to stop at a fence that enclosed a dirt field. From there, we had an unobstructed view of the plaza and platform in the distance. We sat in the midst of a huge crowd. Nicaraguans of all ages sang along with the music that resounded from the plaza. They were ecstatic with excitement. The Pope was to arrive shortly. The crowd waited in anticipation, excited to see and hear "Papa," translated from Spanish as their "reverent father." They hoped and waited for pastoral words of peace.

We stood with the crowd for two hours. Four o'clock came and went. Singing continued, and the crowd remained excited and energized. Five o'clock passed. Finally, at 5:45, cheers from the distance announced the arrival of the Pope. The crowd was elated! When he stepped down from his motorcade, he did not kiss the ground, his common practice. Someone in the crowd yelled, "Kiss our ground, Papa!" The Pope then kissed the ground, walked onto the platform, and announced in Spanish, "I kissed the ground where God has sent me. I salute today the bishops of Nicaragua and the Catholic diocese who have invited me to visit your country."

For the Nicaraguan people, the Mass began as a witness to their undying faith. Their reverence toward the Pope was astounding to watch. "Papa" was truly their messiah on earth. The peaceful celebration as the Mass began was overwhelming; I felt that a ray of hope, like a rainbow, had settled among the people gathered. However, during the Pope's homily, there was no acknowledgment of the Nicaraguan people's past or present suffering. He did not refer to their grief over the youths who had been buried from that same plaza days earlier. Instead, he insisted, "The only way, as Catholics, you can please God is to live and act in unity with your Managua archbishop: Archbishop Obando y Bravo. He and I do not support the Sandinistas who are proponents of 'godless communism.' Archbishop Bravo and I call for peaceful dialogue. We oppose the fermenting ideological revolutionary process that has taken place since the 1979 revolution."

As his homily continued, he stressed the importance of Church unity as the best way to prevent Nicaragua from being corrupted by "godless communism." He spoke out against the growing division within the Church, between the "popular church" that embraces Liberation Theology and the institutional hierarchical Church of "the true" dogma and doctrine. He once again affirmed the Vatican's support for conservative Archbishop Miguel Obando y Bravo and spoke in opposition to the Nicaraguan priests who held government positions.

We listened for some mention of the seventeen youths who had been killed by the contras, or words about the funeral we had attended at the plaza just days before the Pope's visit. The Pope offered no consoling remarks to the mothers and fathers of the fallen youth, who sat in the front row in anticipation of some comforting words. He continued to preach about how Nicaraguans must obey the Church hierarchy. Toward the end of the homily, unable to remain silent, the people began to chant: "Pray for peace, pray for our dead!" "We want a church that stands for the poor!" "We want peace!" "Between Christianity and the revolution, there is no contradiction!" And finally, "Power to the people!" We watched and listened in awe; we were extremely concerned with what had transpired. Would the actions and words solicit a riot?

Suddenly, an angry John Paul II yelled three times, "Silencio! Silencio! Silencio!"

We stood there nervously, astounded that the Pope completely ignored the incident of the youths killed by the contras. The crowd continued their chanting until the Pope, angry with the disruption of the Mass, gave communion to the priests that surrounded him and, without additional words or a blessing, walked off the platform. Nicaraguans, who had joyously and lovingly come to welcome the Pope, cried out in disappointment, "Papa, Papa, Papa!"

We watched as the crowd of seven-hundred thousand left the plaza. We saw the mothers and fathers of the heroes sobbing grievously, tears rolling down their faces as they departed. The Mass had quickly gone from ecclesiastical to political. Even without the coffins, I felt we were attending another memorial service at the July 19 Revolutionary Plaza.

After Margie and her friends departed the platform, Margie came up to our study group, shaking with anger. "I have been holding onto this church by my fingernails; now this, now this!" Margie's anger over the Catholic Church's position on women's ordination and the demeaning patriarchal power at the Mass had taken its toll. She continued, "The Pope could have at least addressed the mothers and fathers of the fallen heroes. Had he, he would have had them and the entire crowd in the palm of his hands. Just a few consoling words, that's all people needed." Our study group gathered around Margie and the other nuns who had sat with her on the platform. United, we all agreed with Margie's words and questioned why the Pope hadn't addressed the mothers and fathers of the fallen youths. We wondered, *was he supporting the contra forces?*

After we returned to our living quarters, friends of Margie's who had attended the Mass joined us to discuss the Pope's visit. The group included directors of the Nicaraguan Christian-based communities, Protestant pastors, the nuns who were our interpreters and guides, and Maryknoll priests and sisters living in Nicaragua. A two-hour discussion helped us understand the outcome of the Pope's visit. A Moravian minister living in Nicaragua explained, "The Pope's visit could set us back years, ecumenically. He does not understand the empowerment, liberation, and reality of the Nicaraguan people. To use 'godless communism' to describe Nicaragua was in error and unfortunate. We are not a 'godless state'!" He addressed our study group. "Please do not make the Pope's homily an issue when you return home. Tell of your other experiences while here. We, as Christians living in Nicaragua, know that what the US government is saying about Nicaragua is a lie!"

Our study group nodded to him in agreement. One of the Maryknoll priests remarked, "The Pope's visit is a significant event in the Nicaraguan Civil War. I believe his visit will deepen tensions between the Sandinistas and the many Nicaraguan Catholics who supported the Sandinistas. The controversial visit will be used by the contras as a form of propaganda to give their organization moral legitimacy. The US administration will capitalize on this event when requesting additional aid for the contra forces. The pontiff does not know all that has happened since the revolution. Rather than helping to alleviate the hierarchy-state tensions, the Pope's visit exacerbated them even more!"

Margie responded, "The Pope stressed the importance of Church unity as the best way to prevent Nicaragua from being corrupted by 'godless communism.' Doesn't he understand the solidarity in the Christian-based communities and the interdenominational work within the revolutionary process that has been extremely effective since the revolution the past four years? I hope he got the crowd's message, 'Between Christianity and the revolution, there is no contradiction.' From our study in Nicaragua, we know that statement is true!"

One of the priests serving in the Sandinista government remarked, "I'm concerned that the Pope advanced the authority of Archbishop Bravo. He affirmed the Vatican's support for conservative Archbishop Bravo and spoke out against the five of us priests who hold government positions. He must think we are corrupted by 'godless communism' also."

One of our guides stated, "We think his visit has convinced us and the vast majority of Nicaraguan people that the Vatican could not be in tune with our problems. When the Pope completely ignored the incident of the youths who were killed, and did not offer any words of condolence for the mothers and fathers of the heroes, he lost his audience."

Margie echoed what we, as a group, were thinking. "I had hoped that the Pope would act as a mediator and support the peace process. He certainly was aware that the Sandinista government used rationed gasoline so that everyone had the opportunity to see him and hear his message. When he spoke out against the growing division within the Church between the 'popular church' and the 'institutional hierarchical church,' he did not understand it was forty years of the hierarchical Somoza dictatorship that ignited the peasants' revolution. That is also why he does not support Liberation Theology. It is neither hierarchical nor patriarchal, but a liberating theology that empowers the poor. It is clear to me that the Pope's homily identified the church hierarchy as a privileged class."

She addressed her Catholic colleagues—the nuns and priest gathered with us. "This is a somber and serious moment for the Catholic Church. I support and commend you sisters and priests for your excellent theology and good works that mandate love, equality, and peace with justice. I leave Nicaragua with renewed hope for a quality life for the people and a sustainable future for Nicaraguans, despite the continued struggle within their daily lives. We will return to the US, tell the truth of the Pope's visit, and demand no more aid to the contras. As a study group, we know the contras are killing innocent people and working to destroy the Sandinista peasants' revolution."

"*L*et my name stand among those who are willing to bear ridicule and reproach for truth's sake, and so earn the right to rejoice when the victory is won."

—Louise May Alcott

Leaving Nicaragua

As we packed, many of us decided to leave our clothes behind, except for what we were going to wear home; AMNLAE could give them to people in need of clothing. We gathered in one room and celebrated a last Nicaraguan meal with our guides. We thanked them for the excellent translation and opportunities that had enhanced our study; we had been provided an excellent education. Each of us believed we were leaving Nicaragua having found the truth.

Before we departed for the airport, we shared our collective writings and reflections. We discussed the slide presentation Margie would create using our words and photos. The communication staff in her New York office would write the script and relate it to slides, so our message throughout the United States would be convincing, powerful, and similar. Each of us agreed to make contact and present our information to the US administration, state department, media, legislative representatives, CWU constituency, churches, human-rights groups, and the United Nations to reveal the truth of our experience.

It was difficult saying our farewells to everyone in Nicaragua who had supported our study. Margie was overcome with emotion when she hugged the nuns and said her goodbyes. We were concerned about the future survival of the people. Would the nuns' lives be additionally threatened following the Pope's visit that had given the contras moral legitimacy?

We boarded our plane, and all of us had tears streaming down our faces as we waved farewell to a people and country we loved. The long silence between Margie and me made me wonder what she was thinking. As our plane ascended into the air, she looked over at me and took my hand in hers. "Sharon, do you remember what I asked you to promise me? I am twenty years older than you. No doubt, I'll die first. Today, I am leaving a part of my heart and soul in Nicaragua. Please never forget this request: when I die, I want my remains brought back to Nicaragua to be interred in a barrio of Managua."

I listened to the sincerity of her desire. "I promise you, Margie. Today, I totally understand your request."

Arriving Home

When we landed in Miami, each of us in the study group scattered to meet our planes that would take us to our respective home destinations. We had created a bond that would not be broken; we realized we would remain connected, regardless of the miles that separated us. We agreed that we had a tremendous amount of work to do—but that we were up to the task!

As my plane landed in Grand Forks, North Dakota, without luggage and only a notebook to carry, I immediately ran to meet my family. Inside the terminal, four faces filled with smiles and tears greeted me. Their embracing hugs warmed me. As we strolled to our car, I felt frozen physically as we walked against a forty-mile-an-hour wind-chill factor, a March winter reality in North Dakota. Having just spent two weeks in above-eighty-degree temperatures, I could hardly wait to get inside our vehicle. I longed for the warmth of my family and to hear the stories I'd missed for two weeks.

Our car was filled with chatter as we traveled the seven miles from the airport to our home. "Grandpa and Grandma went back to Bemidji when we left for the airport, but our supper is ready and homework done," my daughter, Kelly, informed me. They were also excited to tell me that in my absence, they'd learned how to wash their own clothes.

I was delighted that we'd have an entire evening of family time. Over dinner, Mark, Kelly, and Josh each talked about their daily school routine and their moments with Grandma and Grandpa. When they asked about the Nicaraguan children, I did not mention the funeral of the young people; instead, I told them of the night in the barrio when we ate dinner and enjoyed the Nicaraguan families gathered there. I gave them the few *cordobas*—Nicaraguan coins—I brought back so they could take them to show at school. I had no other gifts for them, except a mother's love that ran much deeper than I'd ever previously known.

Once the children went to bed, Gary and I talked extensively about the study tour. We decided the best first audience would be my University of North Dakota colleagues in the humanities department. They knew the issues in Nicaragua, supported my study tour, and opposed contra aid. They would understand and help determine my strategy for telling the story in the future. Gwen Crawford, a staff person in the religious-studies department, was a friend of mine who served on the Grand Forks City Council. I knew I could depend on Gwen, a respected woman on campus, to summon the faculty. It was one week prior to spring break; with a week off from university classes, I'd have time to plan additional options with Margie and the study group.

Home in our own bed, I felt so comforted, especially in the arms of my loved one. In the middle of the night, I shot upright and yelled "*Stop!*" My cry woke Gary from a sound sleep. As he held me, I explained to him, "I was back in Nicaragua yelling at the contras, because I tried desperately to stop them from massacring the youths protecting a Nicaraguan coffee field along the Nicaraguan-Honduran border." I hoped this would be my last nightmarish dream.

The following morning, after the children left for school and Gary for work, I, exhausted from the trip, spent the morning sorting out my thoughts, notes, and future strategies. I called my friend Gwen to ask when would be a good time to talk with her and the faculty. "Come to the religious-studies department this afternoon; everyone is excited to learn about your study tour. I'll arrange everything!"

When I entered the religious-studies department at Merrifield Hall, the room was filled with colleagues. They listened intently to the Nicaraguan story, and then each faculty member asked me to speak in their classes: English, communication, history, religious studies, women's studies, peace studies, philosophy, and social studies. They wanted students to hear the Nicaraguan story prior to spring break. "It will offer them fodder to consider while on the beaches," one of my faculty friends stated. I was elated!

Within four days, the slides and script were available from Margie's New York office. I lectured in eight classes. Students were receptive and asked important questions. Together, we carried on informative discussions. Many had opposed US military involvement in Vietnam and thought that the undeclared Nicaraguan War was similar. Faculty pledged to write the Reagan administration and demand "No more aid to the contras!" Women's studies and peace studies faculty agreed to add the Nicaragua Civil War to their curriculum. Students said that, following spring break, they'd place political signs in their residence halls, requesting "No more military aid to the contras." Gwen, a delegate to the Democratic party caucus meeting, agreed to give what she called a "heart-rendering" speech about the injustices in Nicaragua. Through all of these reinforcing and reaffirming reactions, I gained confidence in telling my story.

"Be the change that you wish to see in the world."

—Mahatma Gandhi

Taking to the Road for Peace with Justice

*M*argie *called on the* first day of spring break to talk about various audiences to engage when discussing our Nicaraguan experience. I told her of my excellent discussion with UND colleagues and the rhetoric that had transpired with students in each class.

"Sharon, let's begin telling our Nicaraguan story in North Dakota. What do you think of a North Dakota State Assembly on wheels? We could market the assembly with the slogan 'Taking to the Road for Peace with Justice.' You live in the 'Peace Garden State.' North Dakota was the first legislative body that passed the resolution for a National Peace Academy; the University of North Dakota held a major peace conference in 1982; UND has added a 'peace studies' minor with an excellent curriculum. If North Dakota seceded from the Union, it would be the third-largest nuclear force in the world. This is an ideal location to launch our Nicaraguan story, don't you agree? I'll help plan an agenda; Church Women United has funds budgeted to fund this pilot project."

I liked the idea immediately. "We'll create a classroom on wheels, Margie. A bus equipped with a microphone, newsprint, a chalkboard, and our Nicaraguan story. It'll work! But I must be able to sell local legislators, our Church Women United constituency, news media, and peace advocates on the idea." When she hung up, I knew my work was just beginning.

Some of the people, when they first heard the state-assembly-on-wheels idea, said it would be impossible; others, that it was *not* impossible—but not too practical, either. However, it did not take long to fill the bus with over thirty North Dakota activists, and two months later, on May 17, 1983, we were "Taking to the Road for Peace with Justice" on a two-day tour throughout the state of North Dakota. Margie was at the helm.

Margie, along with the CWU North Dakota state president and ecumenical action committee, planned the agenda. They coordinated the tour with the realization that "peace with justice" included the concerns of nurturing the human community while promoting justice, creating and becoming caretakers of the earth, advocating advancements for sustainable basic human needs, and respecting our neighbors, both in North Dakota and throughout the world. All these issues would align with a discussion of Nicaragua.

Our first stop, in Grand Forks, was at the LISTEN (Love Is Sharing the Exceptional Needs) drop-in center. The director of the center discussed the socialization of people with varying abilities who utilize the facility. Founded by Grand Forks Church Women United in 1979, the center's program provides education, social activities, and a safe place for people to spend spare time in this home environment, open from 9:00 AM to 9:00 PM daily.

As we traveled from Grand Forks, it became clear to participants why North Dakota, with its productive Red River Valley and sustainable-farming industry, is considered the "breadbasket of the USA": the landscape is covered with rich, black soil, and sugar beets, corn, wheat, sunflowers, potatoes, and numerous other crops grow in this soil-rich farm belt. In May, farmers were lined up in the fields with huge, modern machinery that cost more than most homes. As we traveled, it became evident that farming was an economic engine for North Dakota.

In Fargo, we stopped at the Rape Crisis and Adult Abuse Center. We learned of the education provided at the center to advance women's lives. Their education was to empower them to gain confidence and develop professional skills in the workplace. On our trip from there to Minot, Margie and I discussed with the group our experience with the women at the Ex-Prostitutes Rehabilitation Center in Nicaragua. The participants agreed that women's lives are connected and similar throughout the world.

When we arrived at the Minot Air Force Base, having passed the missile silo "planted" in the wheat field, one of the participants remarked, "Something is wrong with this scene. We're giving birth and death in the same field." At that moment, Margie knew that "Taking to the Road for Peace with Justice" was a great idea. Lieutenant Colonel Phillips, our guide on the base, predicted that the year 2000 would be the "space age" for nuclear testing. One of the participants questioned,

"Who owns outer space, and what effect will nuclear testing have on the ecology of the world?" Lieutenant Colonel Phillips did not have an answer. We knew this would be a good question to discuss on the bus. We agreed, as we traveled the one hundred miles from Minot to Bismarck that war is hell—in either Nicaragua or in the United States.

In Bismarck, the capital city, we met with Governor Olson. He affirmed our work and our support of the National Peace Academy. When we told him about our experience in Nicaragua and asked his position on the contras, he stated, "Your questions make me uncomfortable, but I encourage you to continue making politicians uncomfortable." His statement set us up perfectly for our Nicaragua story. That evening, with a large group of North Dakota legislators, representatives of the North Dakota Conference of Churches, city council members, University of St. Mary College educators, and the general public interested in Nicaragua, Margie and I showed our slides and told our Nicaragua experience. The audience agreed they would relay our story and experience throughout North Dakota, including in their churches, synagogues, town halls, chambers of commerce, and government and legislative offices. They would locate places where large numbers of people frequently gathered. I agreed to speak at upcoming events.

The next morning, before leaving Bismarck, we went to the United Tribes Technical Center, the only Indian-owned and -managed educational facility in the United States. Job placement was 75 percent successful. Of the American Indian population, 80 percent are unemployed and the Bureau of Indian Affairs funding is being decreased rapidly, causing additional economic problems for the Indian population in the state. We informed the director at the technical center that in the 1970s, Church Women United gave sixteen thousand dollars to this center for use by the United Tribes for the women's facility.

From there, we traveled five miles to the North Dakota State Penitentiary, where the director took us on a forty-five-minute tour. We saw furniture, soaps, and craft items being made and sold. We met with one of the counselors, who explained that there were only six counselors for the 415 inmates. The facility was beyond maximum capacity, with an increase of inmates due to a depressed economy. With the high, barbed-wire, razor-sharp fences surrounding the entire property, the exterior scene was extremely different from the rehabilitation prison farm we had visited in Nicaragua.

As we traveled from Bismarck, we discussed the connections between what happens locally that affects people globally. I asked the question, "Wouldn't it be more appropriate for international relations if funding was provided for aiding the human condition instead of spending US tax dollars on war that benefits no one?"

After traveling seven hundred miles throughout the state, meeting numerous people, fostering quality discussions, and examining future strategies, all on the bus realized that "Taking to the Road for Peace with Justice" had worked. Once more, Margie had been right! Participants on the bus and people we met were committed to contacting their local media, meeting with their elected officials, and writing the Reagan administration. I was scheduled to tell the Nicaragua story in ten local communities. When we arrived back in Grand Forks, Margie announced, "I'll work to model this 'state assembly on a bus' in all fifty states, leading up to the CWU international assembly in 1984."

Two years prior to our study tour in Nicaragua, Margie, as director of citizen action for Church Women United, had begun plans to host a CWU global assembly in 1984 at Purdue University in Indiana. She asked if I would serve on the planning committee. On the North Dakota bus, our group discussed the theme for the global assembly: "Come! Build a New Earth: Pieces to Peace." Issues would be global. We agreed that the presence and participation of women representing other countries and cultures would be essential to the global impact of this assembly. International people would share concerns and work with us to help create a just, caring, peaceable world. One of the major focus sessions at the assembly would be the Nicaraguan study-tour experience.

Each state, prior to the international assembly, was asked to sponsor a peace-bus tour that resembled the "North Dakota Taking to the Road for Peace with Justice" event. We hoped the message of the undeclared war in Nicaragua would activate people to meet with their congressional representatives, write the Reagan administration, contact local media, and tell the story in small and large communities.

During 1983, women representing forty of the fifty states agreed to host a pre-assembly bus tour prior to the global assembly in 1984. Margie knew that engaging people throughout each state would be the best way to bring truth to the reality that the United States financing the contras and providing military intervention in Nicaragua was unjust. As director of citizen action for Church Women United and founder of the Coalition to Stop Intervention in Central America, Margie had a large, informed constituency she could activate—and she did!

Although each state had a variety of audiences, the message was the same. Ninety-five percent of the participants who rode the bus for peace with justice, or gathered within their communities to hear the Nicaraguan story, signed up for the International Assembly in 1984 to "Come! Build a New Earth: Pieces to Peace."

Building a New Earth:
Pieces to Peace

"*Come! Build a New* Earth: Pieces to Peace" global assembly was held at Purdue University in West Lafayette, Indiana, July 19–23, 1984. More than two thousand people attended, and sixty countries had sent delegates who were committed to peace building in the global community.

Throughout the five days, focus sessions were held that featured "pieces" of the assembly. The Nicaraguan focus session was titled "Called to be Peacemakers." Margie and those of us who had been on the study tour provided two presentations each day about our Nicaraguan experience. Hours of discussion followed. After telling our story, Dora, my friend from Cuba, talked about her work with the Nicaraguan Literacy Campaign. Soviet women talked about the farm supplies and medical equipment their country had provided for the Nicaraguan people in the beginning of the 1979 revolution. Representatives from Cuba and the Soviet Union described the ways their countries had been active in the agrarian-reform system that had helped activate

Nicaragua's economic development. Women in other countries articulated their concern that the US military intervention in Nicaragua created an unjustifiable war that halted the Sandinista government's ability to get their economy functioning.

The assembly became a global call to informed citizen action. People with similar values had become determined to work together for the same common goals, regardless of their government's positions. We left with renewed hope for a more just future. "Come! Build a New Earth: Pieces to Peace" had provided the global platform for continued discussion, informed decision making, and action.

Following the 1984 Church Women United Global Assembly, communities across the country and within the world population were calling for no more aid to the contras. The twenty-four million dollars earmarked by Congress for the contras was being quickly depleted, due to extensive funding of the contra war. Throughout the world, citizens learned that the US government was also funding the installation of landmines along Nicaraguan harbors; more innocent victims were reported killed due to explosions of the hidden mines. The media reported, as our study group already knew, that the US presence in Nicaragua had become embarrassingly overt. The disclosure that harbors had been mined in Nicaragua by the United States was received badly by the general public and media.

When the Reagan administration proposed an additional twenty-two million dollars in supplemental assistance for the contras, Congress was in doubt as they debated the course of US policy. The uproar over the harbor mining and killing of innocent victims made any future appropriations unlikely. Our study group was elated when House Speaker Tip O'Neil declared, "In my view, the president's funding request for the contras is dead!" However, neither House Speaker O'Neil nor the US Congress knew at that time that President Reagan was so hell-bent on destroying the Sandinistas that he'd established an illegal operation that would supply military aid to the contras, even if it meant trading US hostages for arms.

"Contragate"

The remainder of the Nicaragua-United States story is sad history.* The outcome of President Reagan illegally soliciting the help of the Central Intelligence Agency, along with the hiring of Lieutenant Oliver North, created "Contragate," more officially referred to as "the Iran-Contra affair." The Iran-Contra affair involved a secret foreign policy directed by White House officials in the National Security Council, under President Ronald Reagan. The illegal operation had two goals: first, to sell arms to Iran in the hope of winning the release of US hostages in Lebanon, and second, to illegally divert profits from these sales to the contras fighting to overthrow the Sandinista government in Nicaragua. Margie had articulated concerns over both of these issues, but when we had been studying in Nicaragua, proof of selling arms to Iran for the release of the

---

* The story and findings can be read in the "Report of the Congressional Committees Investigating the Iran-Contra Affair" published in November, 1987. Included in the document is the US Senate Select Committee on Secret Military Assistance to Iran and the Nicaraguan Oppositions and US House of Representatives Select Committee to Investigate Covert Arms Transactions with Iran.

US hostages and diverting profits for these sales to the contras could only be speculated, not proven.

Compared to the Watergate incident, I believe the Contragate scandal was worse for our country. The US government created a secret, covert operation that solicited funds from undisclosed sources outside the United States—this covert activity was accomplished without a vote in the United States Congress; the US government carried out an undeclared war in which innocent victims died at the expense of US tax dollars; the US government mined harbors without the knowledge of Congress; and the US government traded hostages for arms, creating the Iran-Contra affair.

Today, Contragate is an embarrassment written into US—and *world*—history. Viewed alongside Watergate, it reveals the greatest political scandal and presidential abuse of power in US history. The question begs an answer: Why was President Reagan not impeached for Contragate? If President Nixon had not resigned, wouldn't *he* have been impeached for Watergate?

Our study group cannot take full credit for the vote in the US Congress that ended all aid to the contras. However, we can take credit for engaging the masses in local, state, and global communities that, along with the United Nations, demanded the elimination of all military aid to the contras fighting against the Sandinista government.

"The moment we begin to fear the opinions of others and hesitate to tell the truth that is in us, and from motives of policy are silent when we should speak, the divine floods of light and life no longer flow into our souls."

—Elizabeth Cady Stanton

Marching with Margie
and Rosa Parks

*N*icaragua *was at the* forefront of media attention when the Church Women United Citizen Action Committee was holding a meeting in Washington, DC. As a member of the committee, I flew there to spend a week working on important issues. We were to discuss and take action that would demand the return of the US hostages held in Lebanon and work on issues related to apartheid in South Africa, in support of the release of Nelson Mandela from prison.

I hadn't seen Margie for six months, since the global assembly in Purdue, so I was anxious to have these days with her. When I met her at the hotel, I was shocked by her yellowish skin color. I asked her if she felt well. "I'm just exhausted from working on Nicaragua issues. This undeclared war is really hard, tiring work!" she exclaimed.

I asked her if she'd seen a doctor. "Yes, I went to the clinic before I flew to Washington. The doctor said I have jaundice, possibly related to our Nicaraguan trip. I have another appointment when I return to New York."

I had never seen Margie so forlorn. The Nicaraguan issues had taken a toll on her health. I was extremely concerned about her well-being. However, no matter how poor her health, she was still relentless in her work for peace with justice.

Looking over the agenda for the meeting the following day, Margie said, "Sharon, while in Washington, we have another opportunity to work for peace with justice. At Howard University a group is assembled with Rosa Parks, demanding the release of Nelson Mandela and an end to apartheid in South Africa. As you know, since 1948, racial discrimination has been institutionalized through the enactment of apartheid. The penalties imposed on protest—even nonviolent protest—have been severe. Thousands of individuals have died in custody, frequently after gruesome acts of torture. People who were tried were sentenced to death, banished, or imprisoned for life—like Nelson Mandela. He has served over twenty years in a South African prison due to his nonviolent protest against the apartheid system. Our Citizen Action Committee can attend the demonstration later this afternoon and demand Mandela's release. You know how I detest racism! Do you want to go with me?"

After our Nicaraguan experience, I knew this would be another "burden of knowing" event. However, I hated apartheid in South Africa, admired Rosa Parks for her refusal in 1955 to move to the back of the bus, and knew that this was one opportunity to act against racism. "Of *course* I'll go with you, Margie."

When we arrived at the location with our friends, who also served on the Citizen Action Committee, demonstrators were walking in a huge circle, chanting, "Release Nelson Mandela!" The demonstration, organized by Randall Robinson, national coordinator of the Free South African Movement, was held only a few feet from the front door of the South African embassy.

Margie shared her thoughts with our committee. "Rosa Parks and Amy Carter, along with others, got arrested today in an act of civil disobedience. If you cross the line within fifty feet in front of the South African embassy, you will get arrested. Crossing the line is an illegal act. Rosa and Amy crossed the line and rang the doorbell to talk with the ambassador. They wanted to announce their opposition to apartheid. That action will get you arrested."

Along with Margie, eleven of us, members of the CWU Ecumenical Action Committee, began to walk in the circle and chant with the large group of demonstrators. As I strolled along in the circle, I thought of Rosa Parks. Now in her eighties, she was once again willing to be arrested. Her refusal to move to the back of the bus and the ensuing bus boycott brought the fledging civil-rights movement of the twentieth century to national attention. Wasn't apartheid another unjust, racist system, just like the racism that demanded you ride in the back of the bus if born an African American?

Margie whispered, "Sharon, during the 1960s, I marched in Selma, Alabama, against the evils of racism. If Rosa Parks was willing to be arrested again today at her age, so am I. *You* do what feels right for you." I looked at my friends who were walking and chanting with us. They started walking toward the South African embassy behind Margie. I did not hesitate to join them.

The twelve of us began to stroll over to the white line of demarcation. Together, we crossed the line then walked to the front door of the embassy and rang the doorbell. Of course, no one answered. The police came toward us with arrest warrants and handcuffs. Margie asked that she not be handcuffed because with her weight, height, and ill health, she did not think she could walk up the steps into the police paddy wagon. The police obliged her request. The rest of us were handcuffed and, along with Margie, placed in the same vehicle to travel to the police station.

On the way, I recognized how empowering it was to do civil disobedience. I heard my dad's words echo in my head: "There is oftentimes a greater law than the law of the land." I felt proud of our action that I hoped would draw nationwide attention to the unjust system of racial apartheid and inspire Congress to impose economic sanctions against South Africa. As we sang songs of peace on the twenty-minute ride to the police station, "We Shall Overcome" took on a whole new meaning for me. I was grateful to be in the company of such empowered women, determined to help overcome the injustice of racism.

When we were fingerprinted, one of the Catholic sisters in our group gave a handkerchief to the police officer so he could wipe the blood that ran down his cheek. Before we arrived, he had shaved and cut his cheek. After fingerprinting, we were released. The police officer told us that we had to appear in court the following morning.

At 8:00 AM the next day, we sat in a court filled with people arrested for civil disobedience. The judge called the names of the twelve of us; we were all tried at the same time. Each of us pled guilty. We were each charged with a misdemeanor and fined fifty dollars, which seemed a small price to pay. We hoped our act of civil disobedience would help get Nelson Mandela released from prison and put an end to the unjust apartheid system.

That afternoon, I called Gary to tell him about my arrest. He was proud of my stance against racism. When I hung up, I thanked Margie for providing this nonviolent opportunity. The incident with Rosa Parks gave me additional respect for her refusal to move to the back of the bus. Rosa had inspired her pastor, Dr. Martin Luther King, Jr., and had set an example of what one person can accomplish when she or he works and acts on behalf of justice.

When Nelson Mandela was released from prison and elected South Africa's leader, his nonviolent leadership and actions led to the end of apartheid in his country. When elected, Mandela stated, "If I stay angry over the people who put me in prison, they will still have power over me." Now in his nineties, he remains a major influence in South Africa—and around the world.

The Death of Margie

Following our arrest, during five days of CWU Citizen Action Committee meetings, Margie did not feel well. She was totally exhausted; she exhibited the least amount of energy I had ever witnessed during my years working with her. Instead of strolling around the room energizing the committee, she chose to sit. She left Washington early for her doctor's appointment in New York. Our Citizen Action Committee was extremely worried about her health.

When I returned to Grand Forks, she called to tell me that the doctors were performing additional tests. She would know the results in two days. Two days later, she called with the news. "The doctor said the yellow jaundice color of my skin is due to pancreatic cancer, one of the most serious cancers. They are going to perform surgery tomorrow. I'm in the hospital for a preoperative workup.

"A priest came to give me a blessing for the sick, but before he anointed my body, I asked him how he felt about US aid to the contras. He told me that he opposed our government's military intervention in Nicaragua. I let him anoint my body and offer me a blessing." Then she laughed her hearty, Margie laugh.

I laughed along with her. "Margie, even on your sickbed, you carry the torch for justice. What would you have done if he had said he supported US aid to the contras?"

"I would neither have let him offer me a blessing nor anoint me. I would have told him he was not worthy!"

I told her I would fly to New York and be there when she came out of surgery. "I do not want you to come to New York until I'm released from the hospital. I will need your help when I return to my Morningside Garden apartment later."

I told her I loved her, and she responded, "I love you, too, my precious friend."

I tossed and turned all night. The following morning, I was trembling in prayer when the telephone rang. It was Margie's and my good friend Terry. "Margie came through surgery and is in the recovery room. That is all the doctor could tell me, but I'll call as soon as I learn more." I assured Terry I would remain by the telephone.

Two hours later, she called again. "Sharon, I have sad news. Margie just died of a massive heart attack while in the recovery room. You must get a flight and come help us with her death and funeral arrangements. You know her requests."

I could not respond. Grief filled my vocal cords and entire system. I hung up the telephone. Sobbing, I called Gary. "Gary, Margie has died—please come home," I pleaded. Gary cried with me as, together, we threw things in my suitcase and hurriedly prepared for me to leave for Manhattan.

Margie's Funeral

When I arrived at LaGuardia Airport, I dreaded going directly to Margie's apartment. I knew our close friends were all gathered there, but I could not imagine her home without her presence, her stimulating conversation, and her laughter. Her Manhattan apartment defined Margie: Nicaraguan posters, peace signs, books, her art collection, personal belongings, writings, literature, and artifacts that meant the most to her. It was her spiritual dwelling place.

As I entered Margie's apartment, our friends who had gathered there were saddened with disbelief. Sitting in a "Margie circle," a seating arrangement Margie had designed so everyone could face each another as they talked, we all cried together; no one spoke. The room was full of Margie; even her empty coffee cup sat on the kitchen table. Our friend Terry, who had called to tell me of Margie's death, hugged me. She and Margie's friends had spread some of Margie's personal items out on a table. Terry picked up Margie's purple wristwatch. Tears running down her face, she said sadly, "Take this, Sharon, in remembrance of all the special moments

you've shared with Margie. She'd want you to have it."
I was grateful for the sentimental gift. I wanted to wear
Margie's "moments in time" on my wrist. The friends
each took an item that resembled theirs and Margie's
unique relationships.

Gathered in her apartment, each of us took turns
discussing how Margie had affected, influenced, and
empowered our lives. We, her close friends, agreed the
funeral must reflect the totality of Margie's life: her lived
experiences. Her childhood parish church, St. Vincent
Ferrer, in New York, was chosen for the Catholic Mass.
Catholic sisters, friends of Margie's, contacted a priest
whom they and Margie knew well. His theology was
one they embraced. When they called Father John, he
invited them to help him with the funeral Mass.

I informed our friends that, following the funeral
in New York and after her cremation, we must determine a date to take Margie's remains to Nicaragua. "I
promised her that I'd make certain her ashes be taken to
Nicaragua. She wanted them to be interred in a barrio
in Managua. Her request was to be buried among the
martyrs and heroes there." Her friends, many of them
Catholic sisters, knew this was Margie's request, and
they wanted to take Margie's final journey with me.

The night before the service, I went to the funeral
home early, prior to public visitation; I wanted to
make certain Margie looked like herself in the casket.
Lying there without her infectious smile, green, twin-
kling eyes, thunderous voice, and huge hug, the reality
of her death profoundly struck me. She looked even
bigger lying still in the casket than her body did when
she had stomped around a room. After I had combed

and brushed her naturally curly hair as she had always worn it, then wiped most of the pink lipstick that had been applied by the funeral director from her lips, I invited our friends to join me. None of us could believe this bigger-than-life woman was silenced. As we stood by her casket, we all agreed to carry on her work for peace with justice, no matter how difficult the burden.

Over 250 people came to the visitation. The diverse group represented people she had marched with during the civil-rights, women's and peace movements, Catholic nuns who had professionally worked with her since Margie said her vows in 1942, women active in the women's movement, and a large Church Women United constituency. The gathered group represented a variety of cultures, races, and faith groups, all present to pay their respects to Margie. The 250 people collectively were a microcosm representative of the world macrocosm—the most diverse group I'd seen in one location.

The following morning, the large church was filled to capacity with people from throughout the United States and the entire world. I was extremely proud to be a pallbearer.

Before Mass began, a priest representing St. Vincent Ferrer welcomed the five hundred people in attendance. He looked out at the diverse congregation then announced, "Only Catholics can come forward today to receive Holy Communion. The rest of you can come forward, and I'll offer you a blessing."

In a loud voice, Margie's friend Ruth Fitzpatrick, executive director of the Women's Ordination Conference, called out, "You know that's not true! You're *all* welcome to receive Communion." The priest, disgruntled with her words, began Mass with the assistance of Father John. Mass was wonderfully inclusive and was going smoothly until it was time for Communion.

During Communion, Sister Maureen Fiedler, host of the public radio program "Interfaith Voices" and another close friend of Margie, went up and down the aisles announcing, "Everyone, please come to Communion." As she ushered at each pew, almost everyone, Catholics and non-Catholics, lined up to receive Communion.

The all-inclusive funeral service began and ended in an uplifting celebration of Margie's life. Many members of the civil-rights, peace, and women's movements, along with human-rights advocates, shared memories of Margie. They articulated her constant work on behalf of peace with justice. It was exactly as Margie would have wanted.

The language was inclusive and culturally appropriate, women had major roles in the service, and friends spoke of Margie as one widely known for her progressive stands on issues related to the Church and the larger world: poverty, economic justice, classism, equality, racism, sexism, and war. It was uniquely a "Margie Service." Afterward, many of us questioned, "Why can't the Catholic Church, at *all* times, be this inclusively appropriate and theologically correct?" It felt like a breath of fresh air had finally risen above us and cleaned out the stale, moldy basement that housed patriarchy.

At the close of the celebrative service, when we sang, "Let There Be Peace on Earth," I could hear Margie's thunderous voice resounding at the top of her lungs. When the service concluded and we carried her coffin out of the church, the congregation continued, "Let there be peace on earth, and let it begin with me." I knew at that moment that Margie was nodding her head up and down: "Yes, of course!" Our friend, Professor Ada Maria Isasi Diaz, innovator of Hispanic Theology, bent down and whispered alongside the head of the casket, "I hope you're singing in Spanish as I taught you, Margie."

Later, a conservative Catholic publication, *Living Traditions*, reported Margie's funeral:

> In the Church of St. Vincent Ferrer, feminist friends crowded around the altar of sacrifice. In the words of feminist Ruth McDonough Fitzpatrick, executive director of the Women's Ordination Conference, "At the consecration, the priest on the altar was surrounded with women. He was trying to elbow them back to give him his sacred space. But all of us extended our hands and said the words of consecration.

The publication concluded:

> In the best circumstances, a celebrating priest has a delicate task in defending himself from the "wickedness and snares of the Devil."

After I read the article, I was amused by the analysis. Many of the women described were Catholic sisters, like Margie, with doctoral degrees in theology and working constantly with people of poverty, teaching and mandating peace with justice. I could imagine Margie's response to the article: "Any type of discrimination on gender is contrary to Jesus' request of equality for all humankind."

"*If* the first woman God ever made was strong enough to turn the world upside down all alone, these women together ought to be able to turn it back and get it right side up again."

—Sojourner Truth

Nicaragua:
Margie's Final Journey

A month after Margie's funeral, twelve of her close friends, including four from the former study group, left for Nicaragua. The flight to Nicaragua carrying Margie's remains was very different from the trip three years earlier, although we took the same route, landing in Belize, Honduras, and finally Nicaragua. We were carrying school supplies Margie had collected for the orphanage.

When we got off the airplane, soldiers surrounded us and sent us directly to immigration officials. At customs, they went through our supplies then questioned why we brought commodities to the children. "Why do you give us charity? Don't you know that it was your government that depleted our economy with an unjustifiable war? Now, as a result, we're left to suffer in abject poverty! These supplies are an insult to us!"

I knew their accusation was true. One of the nuns traveling with us, a Spanish interpreter, told us to wait until an AMNLAE member joined us at customs. A few minutes later, an AMNLAE representative, whom we had met on our former visit, came to our rescue. She stated to the soldiers, "These women represent the Sister Margie Tuite delegation. They have come to Nicaragua to bury her remains in the barrio of Managua as she requested. Margie collected these school supplies, sheets, and medications for the orphanage, as she promised the mothers of the heroes and martyrs." The immigration officials remembered Margie and her previous visits. They let us through without any more questions. We thanked the AMNLAE representative for intervening on our behalf. After helping us with our luggage, she loaded our things in the van for our trip to the orphanage.

The twelve of us traveled with the AMNLAE representative to the orphanage, where the mothers of the heroes and martyrs were gathered. They showed us the van Margie had raised money for to transfer children to and from school. We gave them the supplies and an engraved plaque with Margie's name and photo on it. The director of the orphanage responded, "The children will learn of Sister Margie Tuite and her values during their education. They will be taught how to react against war and work for peace with justice."

One of the mothers of the heroes and martyrs thanked us for the supplies then confided, "Our spirits have dimmed. We feel more hopeless due to the continued war against us. Now, we all grieve Margie's death. She was our hope for the future. Maybe Margie was tired, so God took her home, along with our daughters and sons, to enjoy the reign of God. It's up to the rest of us to carry on Margie's work. In her memory, we must all arm ourselves against US intervention in our country.

Go back and tell Reagan to stop his aggression!" Filled with guilt and grief, our group knew that, in Margie's memory, we must mandate Reagan to stop the military support and aid for the contra forces.

That evening, we gathered with AMNLAE members, who had provided us rooms at a hotel in Managua; we discussed the memorial service that would take place the following day. They informed us that there would be a gathering with the mothers of the heroes and martyrs before the funeral procession would begin. The mothers wanted to walk with us to the memorial service that would take place in a Christian-based community within Managua. A Catholic Mass would be celebrated by the Maryknoll Sisters and priests, friends of Margie's, whose ashes would be on the altar, along with a photo of her that featured her hearty smile.

The following morning, around 10:00 AM, we gathered with the mothers of the heroes and martyrs. The Maryknoll priests we had met at the educational and cultural centers in 1983 were there, along with the nuns who had been guides and interpreters for the study group. We walked and joined the huge crowd of people gathered for the memorial service. Nicaragua had not changed dramatically in the two years since our last visit. Walking with the huge group of young and old people carrying Sandinista flags reminded me of the similar walk when we had gone to hear the Pope at the plaza.

As Margie had requested, we carried her ashes and journeyed through five of the small villages where she had previously worked with local women struggling with poverty. In each village, additional people joined us, until hundreds of somber faces were seen walking and paying their respects to the woman they considered their hero.

I decided to walk barefoot the ten kilometers to her final resting place. My friends cautioned me about how difficult it would be if I cut my feet on glass particles on the dirt roads, but I wanted to feel the earth under my feet; it made me feel more connected to Margie. As we walked, each of us took turns carrying her ashes. When it was my turn, my friend Judy said, "Sharon, carry Margie—as *she* carried *you* through life."

Slowly walking, I felt the hot, dry soil under my feet. As soon as I took Margie's container of ashes, my feet quit burning. Both of my hands wrapped around the urn became extremely warm, almost hot. What was she telling me? At that moment, I knew. Margie's spirit was definitely among and within us. The burden of knowing she had provided me would be Margie's and my legacy for a lifetime.

As we continued to walk, people along the roadside joined the journey to the memorial site. When we arrived at the Christian Base Community where Margie's service was held hundreds of people jammed in close to the altar, their faces solemn with grief. I was overwhelmed by the love the Nicaraguan people showed for Margie; the evident grief for their beloved "hero." As the Mass began, tears flowed from the eyes of all gathered. The Spanish Mass, using Liberation Theology, was a celebration of Margie's life. There was no mention of who could or could not partake of Communion in this ecumenical environment. All were welcome to come forward for the Eucharist. The story of John and Peter with the lame man (Acts 3:11) became the main story during the homily. The message was that the apostles had not given the lame man money, but they gave him dignity. It became the story of what the apostle Sister Margie Tuite had given the Nicaraguan people: their dignity. She had worked for the poor of Nicaragua—for dignity and justice, requesting that Nicaraguans determine their own destiny.

After the Mass, each person, eyes filled with tears, walked to the altar and paid their last visit to Margie's urn and photo. It was heartbreaking to witness their sorrow for the woman who had given them so much hope for the future. Over three hundred people watched as Margie's urn, holding her ashes, was placed in the ground at the barrio in Managua. A grave marker would be placed later that stated: "Sr. Marjorie Tuite: Our Hero and Martyr. 'May She Rest In Peace.'"

Twenty-Six Years Later

Dear Margie:

Where are you? If it is true, as you often proclaimed, "God lives at the juncture of justice," I am certain you are there.

In our lifetime together, you taught me volumes about myself, humankind, and the world. What I learned from you created in me the burden of knowing that continues to haunt my thoughts today, twenty-six years after your departure from this earth on June 28, 1986.

I want to tell you about some important events that have taken place in the world. I imagine that where you are now, you're much better informed to provide me with answers. Whatever the circumstances, it feels good to share some thoughts with you.

How often I hear your provocative voice; see your radiant smile; read your words of wisdom; and long for our personal, political, social, and theological conversations. I miss the love you provided me and my family; and Gary, Mark, Kelly, and Josh miss you, too.

We desperately need your values engaged in the

world's reality today. I know you would demonstrate that working for peace with justice is the way to enhance the human condition. Certainly, you would try to prove once again that dominion, mastery, and war are not the way to shape our world.

First in this letter, I want to reiterate news of Nicaragua, where I left your remains in 1986. Remember, while we were studying there, you suspected the United States was selling arms to Iran? Later, we read in the November 3, 1985, Lebanese weekly *Al-Shiraa* report that the United States had secretly sold arms to Iran. Well, after you left us, subsequent reports concretized that news. Each news release claimed that the purpose of those sales was to win the release of American hostages in Lebanon. Similar to the responses when we reported our Nicaraguan story, some people thought these arms-sales reports were totally false. But *you* knew the truth, didn't you?

The US military is no longer in Nicaragua; Congress has ended all funding to the contras. Currently, Daniel Ortega is the Sandinista leader. After three terms, he was reelected again in 2011, with his campaign promise to please the poor and working classes in Nicaragua. President Ortega has tried to convince the people that his new term in office is an extension of the Sandinista Revolution, but reports indicate that not all Nicaraguans agree. Some are concerned he is exhibiting too much power. Although the country is still experiencing poverty, news reports reveal an indomitable spirit coupled with a great hope for a brighter future void of US military intervention.

I am proud of your successful efforts that discontinued US military intervention in Nicaragua. In 1986, the World Court did find the United States guilty of the terrorist war in Nicaragua, but the US simply refused to recognize the Court.

Ortega and his wife, Rosario Murillo, were recently married in the Catholic Church and received the blessings of former archenemy Cardinal Obando y Bravo. Evidently with the Pope's blessing, Bravo has been promoted from archbishop to cardinal. Possibly, Bravo got the message at the Pope's Mass in Managua, "Between the revolution and Christianity, there is no contradiction."

One of the biggest changes since your time on earth took place September 11, 2001. Militants associated with an Islamic extremist group known as al-Qaeda hijacked four airliners and carried out suicide attacks against the United States. Two of the planes were flown into the towers of the New York City World Trade Center. A third plane hit the Pentagon, just outside Washington, DC, and the fourth plane crashed into a field in Pennsylvania. These attacks resulted in extensive deaths and destruction. The turmoil within the United States created chaos unlike any I had previously witnessed in this country.

Since the September 2001 attacks, the "War on Terrorism" has become a title used consistently in the media and among individuals. Over three thousand people were killed during the attacks in New York City and Washington, DC, including more than four hundred police officers and firefighters. Allegedly, the terrorists were acting in retaliation for America's support of Israel, US involvement in the Persian Gulf War, and continued military presence in the Middle East.

Following the attacks, the United States experienced sympathy, support, and sincere concern within the United Nations and around the entire world. It was heartwarming to witness this worldwide love and support given to American citizens.

However, the US president, George W. Bush, convinced Congress, his staff, and a majority of the American public that Iraq had weapons of mass destruction and might be aligned with Osama bin Laden, instigator of the September 11 attacks. On March 20, 2003, the United States invaded Iraq. No weapons of mass destruction were ever found by the United Nations' weapons inspectors.

Margie, the outcome has been devastating! A September 2010 article in the *Washington Post* reported 4,804 casualties. The cost of the seven-year Iraq War has been over three trillion dollars, leaving the United States with its largest debt since the Great Depression. The American Dream—work hard, and you'll succeed—has been weakened; it is harder to get ahead today, and we are no longer considered the world's greatest-opportunity society.

Susan Jacoby, author of *The Age of American Unreason*, suggested in her book, published in 2008, that the type of media hype that caused the invasion of Iraq is due to our descent into intellectual laziness and our flight from reason, which we have lost as individuals and as a nation. She believes that American citizens today want "infotainment" in the media instead of factual information and states that *foremost* among the victors of anti-intellectualism are the mass media. Writing about the war in Iraq, Jacoby asks this of her readers: "The real question is not why politicians have lied to the public, but why the public was so receptive and so passive when it heard the lies?" Doesn't that sound like the same questions we asked while studying in Nicaragua?

After nine years, in June 2011, Osama bin Laden, the mastermind behind the September 11 attacks, was killed by US forces in a hideout in Pakistan. Current US president Barack Obama, who orchestrated the killing of Osama bin Laden, has recently withdrawn US military troops from Iraq. The outcome of the war and Iraq's future welfare are still questionable. As you constantly reminded me, Margie, "Under any circumstances, war is hell!"

The 2012 presidential campaign is underway, with Republicans trying to defeat Democratic President Obama. A US Supreme Court decision instituted last year removes limits on the amount of campaign contributions that can be made to any one candidate. I know if you were here, you would provide grassroots leadership to support a constitutional amendment that would reverse this unjustifiable Supreme Court decision. As you often suggested, and I concur, our country needs term limits for elected officials; campaign financing is totally out of control!

The voting public today is defined as either "liberal" or "conservative," with no definition between the two titles. Democrats are liberal. Republicans are conservative. What seems strange to me is that many of us went to liberal arts universities to acquire an education that taught us how to adapt and learn over our lifespan. Discussion and difference of opinion were considered attributes in these universities that housed liberal think tanks. I suggest that additional definitions are important to the campaign rhetoric, don't you think? Whatever happened to the word "Moderate"?

Margie, you always worked hard for equality. Unfortunately, the Equal Rights Amendment has still not been ratified in the United States; however, Title IX has been enacted, which offers the opportunity for women to participate in sports. It has been a joy to watch our five granddaughters participate in the sports of their choice. You always advocated equal pay for equal work; however, women are still marginalized in the workplace. According to the April–May 2012 issue of *BookWomen*, published by Minnesota Women's Press, "nationally, women on average earn 77 cents to each dollar earned by men."

You were also a leading voice for equality in the Catholic Church. Women are still not able to be ordained to the priesthood. Currently, there is a new dynamic taking place. A Gallup Poll conducted in 2005 reported a record shortage of priests in the American Catholic Church. The poll found that 63 percent of American Catholics support allowing priests to marry. Fifty-five percent said women should be allowed to become priests. *US News & World Report* stated that perhaps there is no more immediate concern among Catholic leaders than that of adequate Church leadership. My hope is that the Church patriarchy will determine the inequality perpetuated by ordaining only men and validate the dynamic leadership provided by Catholic nuns.

Nuns, many of them your friends, continue their struggle for leadership equality in the Catholic Church. The *New York Times* headline published June 5, 2012, stated, "Nuns, Rebuked by Rome, Plan Road Trip to Spotlight Social Issues." This month, Sister Simone Campbell, a lawyer and executive director of Network, the social-justice lobby in Washington, has organized "Nuns on the Bus." Nuns are traveling to protest federal budget cuts in programs for poor and working families. The federal budget cuts were passed by the House of Representatives and proposed by Paul D. Ryan, a Wisconsin Republican who cited his Catholic faith to justify the cuts.

Sister Campbell stated in the news article: "We're doing this because these are life issues. And by lifting up the work of Catholic sisters, we will demonstrate the very programs and services that will be decimated by the House budget." The nuns believe that half of Ryan's budget facts are 100 percent wrong. The nine-state bus tour started in Iowa and will end in Virginia. I have appreciated their initiatives and watched them, in the media, proclaim, "Catholic sisters across the country work every day with people struggling at the economic margins. Meanwhile, the House of Representative has approved the 'Ryan Budget,' which will harm millions of the people we serve."

I know you'd be riding with the nuns on the bus if you were here, Margie. The signage, "Nuns on the Bus: Nuns Drive for Faith, Family, Fairness," reminds me of our 1983 Church Women United "Taking to the Road for Peace with Justice" bus tour in North Dakota. I hope the nuns' outcome is as rewarding as ours was.

Your dear friend, Sister Maureen Fiedler, currently is host of the hour-long, award-winning, public-radio show "Interfaith Voices." Her National Public Radio broadcast provides interfaith dialogue with people from many faith traditions. This week, I heard her discuss issues on a CBS talk show that I know will interest you. On *CBS This Morning*, speaking with show hosts Gayle King and Charlie Rose, Maureen talked about the Vatican's recent criticism about the majority of US religious women who are politically involved with social-justice issues. Evidently, as a reprimand, the Vatican has chosen an archbishop and two bishops to revise the nun's handbooks, examine their work in, and outside of, the church, and challenge their theological positions on social-justice issues. Sr. Maureen stated, "This issue is a lot more than the Vatican versus the nuns. This is about what kind of Catholic Church we're going to be. When I hear that Vatican mandate for us, what I hear is the voice of the church in the nineteenth century, before the reforming council, the Second Vatican Council of the 1960s."

When Maureen was asked by CBS host Charlie Rose what she thought it would take for nuns to have an equal role and voice in the Catholic Church of the future, she stated "Vatican III!" She sounded so much like you, Margie. I was shocked when she stated on the program that the second-largest Christian denomination in the United States is ex-Catholics. She believes archaic patriarchal control and mandated pre-Vatican II rules are the major reasons people are leaving the church. This comment resonates with her resounding voice at your funeral, when she invited all your friends to partake of Communion.

Our friend Rosa Parks has also departed from this world. I hope she is there with you. As workers against racism while on earth, I know both you and Rosa celebrated the election of the first black US president, Barack Obama, along with the former election of Nelson Mandela as leader in South Africa.

I am writing this book dedicated to you, Margie, because you were the mentor in my life during my younger years. Today, my hope for a more enlightened future resides in the wisdom of people like you and Sister Hildegard of Bingen. I believe that someday, you two will be featured among the world's wisest women. It is refreshing for me to reflect on your and Hildegard's creation-centered spirituality that embraces the belief that we are all born as an original *blessing*, instead of the fall-redemptive Augustinian theology that teaches we are all born as an original *sin*. I suggest the beginning of life for all humankind would have a more holistic origin if we viewed each person on our journey as a blessing.

Margie, there is no sufficient way to thank you for all you have added to my life. This book will hopefully provide opportunities for our friends to reclaim their moments in time with you. It is up to us, is it not, to fulfill your goals and work toward making this a more preferred, pluralistic world for all? On behalf of our six grandchildren, I am committed to continuing your heritage.

In retirement, I have time, energy, and determination for the task, but the "burden of knowing" is not easy! I believe that the hope for the future resides in your legacy.

Until we meet again, dearest friend, I want you to know I love and miss you.

—Sharon

Author's suggested related readings

Jacoby, Susan. *The Age of American Unreason*. New York: Pantheon, 2008.

Maddow, Rachel. *Drift*. New York: Crown Publishers, 2012.

Report of the Congressional Committees Investigating the Iran-Contra Affair With Supplemental, Minority, and Additional Views. November 1987.

U.S. Senate Select Committee on Secret Military Assistance to Iran and the Nicaraguan Opposition.

U.S. House of Representatives Select Committee to Investigate Covert Arms Transactions with Iran.

U.S. Government Printing Office, Washington, D.C.

Sharon Rezac Andersen

Sharon Rezac Andersen is retired as former director of the University of North Dakota International Centre, Grand Forks, North Dakota, where she spent the majority of her professional life academically working with international students, Fulbright scholars, and study aboard programs. She completed a master of fine arts degree in communication with a minor in social psychology at UND. As an undergraduate student majoring in religious studies, philosophy, and women studies, Rezac Andersen studied abroad in Cuba and Nicaragua, and was invited by the USSR Russian Orthodox Church to study Soviet religions, governmental and educational systems. She represented the United Nations Non-Governmental Interchurch Centre in the Czech Republic, her paternal country, at a conference focused on formulating world peace initiatives, studying comparative educational systems and examining the world military complex.

Highlights that sustain Rezac Andersen's fulfilled life include: gathering around the dining table eating and conversing with family and friends; reading, writing, discussing the great books, and enjoying unique special moments with grandchildren: Alexa, Jessica, Kayla, Linsey, Palmer, and Zoë.

She and her husband, Gary, reside in Green Valley, Arizona winter months and Park Rapids, Minnesota during the summer.

Isn't it the responsibility for each of us to repair the pieces of injustice that hinder world peace?

CPSIA information can be obtained at www.ICGtesting.com
Printed in the USA
BVOW011440170213

313456BV00001B/4/P